CRIMINAL LAW

Private Law Tutor Publishing
Foreword

Thank you for buying this book. The problem that I encountered when studying law is: knowing everything. There is so much to read and so little time to do it. If you skip some material, or a case you are none the wiser. So throughout my years teaching law I have devised a system and I am going to share this with you.

You may have encountered different methods or formulas to help when advising a client in a mock scenario. One of example is the *IRAC* method or another is *Celo*. These are well documented and you can read about these. I never used them, because I had a method in my head that worked. It was not until I started teaching that I spoke about it. I call my method the "**Fact Law Sandwich**". Let me explain. If you are asked to advise a party as to their legal rights this is how you present it:

FACTS
GENERAL PRINCIPLE
LAW
APPLY TO FACTS

In **Fact**: simply state what you have been told, this why you can never be accused of not considering the facts. In **General principle:** you simply state what the general rule of the relevant issue is. You express it as if you are speaking to a child who has no knowledge of law. In **Law**: you state "using the authority of…..and you go on to state which statute or case helps prove your point. Lastly in **Apply to Facts**: you apply the reasoning of the case to your factual scenario. Your advice will sound and look structured and professional. The reason it is called the "Fact Law Sandwich", is because the advice contains two outer layers of facts that sandwich the principle and law in the middle.

This book is written to provide the student with a good knowledge of the most important cases on their study. It is written in a way to facilitate the Fact Law Sandwich method. I provide the general principle, the name of the case with full citation, the facts, the Ratio (the thing the lecturers say you always need to use), and application i.e. how the case should be applied. No other book provides this information at your fingertips. I hope you enjoy using it.

CRIMINAL LAW
Private Law Tutor Publishing

Welcome/Introduction/Overview

This book provides you with basic information as a basis for you to form your own critical opinions on this area of law. Once you have mastered the basics, you will be inspired to question contract principles in your essays and apply them in mock client advisory scenarios. Again, for your convenience, we have published a Q&A book that specifically provides you with examples of how to answer such questions and how to apply your knowledge as effectively as possible to help you get the best possible marks.

This aid is a fully-fledged source of basic information, which tries to give the student comprehensive understanding for this module. However, it is recommended that you compliment it with the further reading suggestions provided at the end of each topic, as well as read the cases themselves for more in-depth information. This book provides an analysis of the basic principles of Criminal Law. The following is a summary of the Book content:

- An introduction to Criminal Law;
- What the Criminal Law in England seeks to achieve;
- The legal-philosophical development of criminal law;

The aim of this Book is to:

- Provide an introduction to anyone studying or interested in studying Law to the key principles and concepts that exist in English Criminal Law.
- To provide a framework to consider Criminal Law within the context of examinations.
- Provide a detailed learning resource in order for legal written examination skills to be developed.
- Facilitate the development of written and critical thinking skills.
- Promote the practice of problem solving skills.
- To establish a platform for students to gain a solid understanding of the basic principles and concepts of Criminal Law, this can then be expanded upon through

confident independent learning.

Through this Book, students will be able to demonstrate the ability to:

- Demonstrate and articulate the core principles of Criminal Law and its basic structure and workings.
- Critically assess challenging mock factual scenarios and be able to pick out legal issues in various areas of Criminal Law.
- Apply their knowledge when writing a formal assessment.
- Present a reasoned argument and make a judgment on competing viewpoints.
- Make use of technical legalistic vocabulary in the appropriate manner.
- Be responsible for their learning process and work in an adaptable and flexible way.

Studying Criminal Law

Criminal Law is one of the seven core subjects that the Law Society and the Bar Council deem essential in a qualifying law degree. Therefore, it is vital that a student successfully pass this subject to become a lawyer. Additionally, a knowledge and understanding of criminal law principles is needed in order to study other law subjects such as Public and Administrative, Constitutional, Jurisprudence and legal theory, Human Rights, EU, and International law. You will be given essay questions in your assessments and examinations, so it is vital you are able to fully interpret the law and theory of any area, think in such a way that allows you to analyse it critically and creatively, and articulate it all academically yet understandably. The methods by which these types of question should be approached are somewhat different.

Tackling Problems and Essay Questions

There are various ways of approaching problem questions and essay questions. We have provided students with an in-depth analysis with suggested questions and answers at the end of each chapter.

Chapter 1 - Introduction to Criminal Law

Criminal law protects society's interpretation of right and wrong and deems these acts/ crimes as unlawful which are created to protect the society as whole, individual interests and certain property rights. Any crime is regarded as a 'public wrong' and the State is charged with the responsibility of protecting the moral foundation of the society.

Criminal law is constantly evolving. The changing mind-set of the society results in a corresponding change in law. Most recently there has been a complete change in the sexual offences law, also old offences have been replaced by completely new offences. Amendments are being made every day.

GENERAL PRINCIPLES OF CRIMINAL LAW

There must be a balance between the need to protect the society against unlawful behaviour and the human rights of the accused. Hence, whenever there is an alleged breach of law, the accused will be considered innocent until proven guilty. He must be given a fair trial and the burden of proof lies on the prosecution.

THE BURDEN AND STANDARD OF PROOF

The case of **Woolmington v DPP** [1935] AC 462 laid down the foundation of criminal law. The prosecution has to prove every element of the crime beyond a reasonable doubt. Moreover, Article 6(2) of the ECHR supports this, it provides that 'a person charged with a criminal offence shall be presumed innocent until proven guilty according to the law'.

In exceptional circumstances, the defendant bears the burden to prove a fact on a balance of probabilities test, instead of just adducing evidence of it. Moreover, more exceptional categories are made by the Parliament, but these statutory restrictions must be handled cautiously, as all of them must comply with Article 6(2).

CLASSIFICATION OF OFFENCES

The tribunal that will hear the offence is decided by the classification of the offence. Some offences are more serious than the others.

SUMMARY OFFENCES

These offences are the least serious of all crimes. These offences if committed by an adult are only tried summarily. The Criminal Justice Act, 1988 has made summary only a few offences: common assault, battery and taking vehicles without consent. They are tried only in the Magistrates' Court. The maximum punishment that can be imposed is currently 12 months' imprisonment and a £5,000 fine.

INDICTABLE ONLY OFFENCES

An 'indictable' offence means an offence, which when committed by an adult, is only triable on 'indictment', even though it is exclusively so triable or triable either way. Offences are made indictable only due to the gravity of the crime or some other reason like complexity of the issues involved which makes them unsuitable to be tried as summary offences. These offences include any crime punishable by imprisonment for life on conviction, death caused by dangerous driving and other serious offences under the Theft Act 1968.

An indictable offence is tried by jury and a judge in the Crown Court and the maximum punishment is imposed by the regulating statute. Examples: robbery, rape, murder, manslaughter, causing grievous bodily harm with intent and blackmail.

EITHER- WAY OFFENCES

There are certain offences where the seriousness of the crime depends on the facts of the case. These are classified as 'either way' offences and can either be tried in the Magistrates' Court or in the Crown Court. This decision is initially made by the Magistrates, in whose court the criminal case proceedings commence. If the Magistrate is of the opinion that his powers are sufficient to deal with the case then the case will be tried summarily, although the defendant has the right to choose trial by jury. Contrastingly, if the Magistrate is of the opinion that the case attracts a penalty beyond the Magistrate's power then the case goes to the Crown Court and the defendant loses the right to choose a trial by jury. Example: burglary, theft and unlawful wounding.

THE OBJECTIVES OF CRIMINAL LAW

A useful explanation of the purpose of criminal law was provided by the American Law Institute when they attempted to define the objectives of the criminal law in Article 1 of their Draft Model Penal Code:

(a) to forbid and prevent conduct that unjustifiably and inexcusably inflicts or threatens substantial harm to individual or public interests;

(b) to subject to public control persons whose conduct indicates that they are disposed to commit crimes;

(c) to safeguard conduct that is without fault from condemnation as criminal;

(d) to give fair warning of the nature of the conduct declared to be an offense;

(e) to differentiate on reasonable grounds between serious and minor offenses.

THE BASIC ELEMENTS OF A CRIME

Once the offence has been identified, we need to identify the requirements to establish the offence. The Latin maxim *actus non facit reum nisi mens sit rea* clearly explains the basic elements of criminal liability. A person is not criminally liable for his conduct unless the required state of mind coincides with the prohibited *actus reus.*

ACTUS REUS

This phrase is usually used to describe the act of the accused which is prohibited by law. The concept may also cover omissions or state of affairs. This is an essential element of any offence. Offences may be categorized in several different ways:

- **CONDUCT OFFENCES**

Some offences only require certain acts to be committed by the accused to satisfy the *actus reus*. For instance, fraud by false misrepresentation simply requires the defendant to make a misleading or untrue representation. Even damaging consequences from this action are not important.

- **RESULT OFFENCES**

In such offences, the action of the defendant must result in a specific consequence to satisfy the *actus reus* element. For instance, in the case of murder where the actions of the accused lead to the death of the victim what needs to be proved is that the action caused the result.

- **SURROUNDING CIRCUMSTANCES**

In certain offences, in addition to an action (and a specific result in some cases) surrounding circumstances also form a part of the *actus reus*. For instance, under the Theft Act 1968, appropriation of property under Section 1(1) involves property 'belonging to another'. What needs to be proved here is that the action of the Defendant of allegedly appropriating property was done in circumstances that it 'belongs to another', someone other than the thief.

- **OMISSIONS**

In certain situations, the *actus reus* can be fulfilled when the Defendant has taken no action whatsoever. Criminal law, in certain situations, imposes criminal liability when there is a failure or omission to act. This will be discussed in the subsequent chapters.

MENS REA

This is the second important element of criminal liability. Most offences require that the accused not only commit an act but that action must be accompanied by a 'guilty mind'. The term *'mens rea'* covers a variety of mind states that need to be proved in relation to the *actus reus* of the crime in question. In some offences, a particular *actus reus* may require more than one type of *mens rea* in order to establish that offence.

Some offences use other words when defining *mens rea*, for instance they can use the term 'maliciously'. This denotes that the *actus reus* must be committed intentionally or recklessly (for example Section 20 of the Offences Against the Person Act 1861).

General Principle: Contrastingly, some offences do not require *mens rea* in every element of the offence.

Cundy v LeCoq (1884) LR 13 QBD 207
Facts: The Defendant was convicted for selling liquor to a drunken person that was against Section 13 of the Licensing Act1872. The Defendant had no means of knowing that his customer was drunk. Moreover, the section did not have any requirements that referred to the Defendant's knowledge, or that the Defendant should ascertain that the customer was drunk or not. **Ratio: The issue for the court was whether awareness of the customer's condition had to be taken into consideration according to the wording of the Statute. Whether the answer was no, the element of *mens rea* should have not needed to be proven. Application:** By looking at the wording of the Statute the prohibition was held to be absolute and the Defendant convicted. His knowledge of the condition of the customer was not necessary to constitute the offence. The court allowed the application of the so-called 'strict liability' even though the Defendant alleged to have committed a bona fine mistake. The court took into consideration the absence of the required *mens rea* as a matter of mitigation of the penalties but not as an element that allowed avoidance of liability.

CO-INCIDENCE OF ACTUS REUS AND MENS REA

The prosecution needs to establish that the *actus reus* and *mens rea* occurred at the same time. This will be studied in more detail in chapter 3.

SUMMARY

- Criminal law protects individuals and their property from harm, preserves order in society, punishes those that commit offences.

- The accused will be considered innocent until proven guilty.

- The burden of proof lies with the prosecution.

- There are different potential offences.

- Offences may be described as summary (the least serious), indictable (whether they require a jury in front of the Crown Court) or either-way offences.

- Criminal law aims to forbid and prevent unlawful actions, protect the general public and give guidance on what is lawful and what is not.

- The basic elements of a crime are the *actus reus* and the *mens rea*.

- The actus reus element may constitute in a conduct, result, omission.

- The *mens rea* element is represented by the status of the Defendant's mind.

Chapter 2 - Homicide
Actus Reus & Causation: Murder

INTRODUCTION

Under English law, homicide is used as a generic term which covers causing the death of another human being. Murder is the most serious kind of homicide and the distinguishing factor is that the defendant must act with a specific intent. Following the Murder (Abolition of Death Penalty) Act 1965, it is punished by a mandatory life sentence. The judge does not have any discretion in sentencing other than to consider a minimum term before a prisoner can be released on license.

DEFINITION OF MURDER

There is no statutory definition of murder. The definition laid down by Sir Edward Coke is still applicable today:

> *"Murder is committed when a man of sound memory, and of the age of discretion, unlawfully kills within any county of the realm any reasonable creature in being under the King's peace, with malice aforethought either expressed by the party or implied by law, so as the party wounded or hurt die of the wound or hurt within a year and a day after the same."*

Hence, the major elements of murder are: the killing must be unlawful; the victim of the homicide must be a person (being) and must be under the jurisdiction of the United Kingdom. Hence, it can be committed anywhere in the UK or on any British ship or aircraft.

ACTUS REUS

The *actus reus* of murder is satisfied when certain elements are fulfilled. The killing must be unlawful. It is lawful to kill another person, for example, when enemy soldiers are killed during battle, in cases of death penalty and in self-defence.

General Principle: The victim of the homicide must be a person.

Attorney-General's Reference [1996] 2 All ER 10
Facts: A man stabbed his pregnant girlfriend in the abdomen. She gave birth prematurely, and the baby died some four months later as a result of its immaturity. The Defendant was acquitted of murder at the judge's direction and the Attorney-General referred various points of law to the Court of Appeal. **Ratio: Lord Taylor CJ said the elements of the *actus reus* of murder are that the defendant did an act, that was intentional rather than accidental, that was unlawful, that was a substantial cause of the death of a person in being and (as the law then stood) that the death occurred within a year and a day of the act. The *mens rea* is that at the time of the act the Defendant intended either to kill or to cause really serious injury to the victim or (subject to the extent of transferred malice) to some other person. The House of Lords subsequently reversed Lord Taylor's judgement as to the applicability of transferred malice in this case and disagreed with his suggestion that the foetus could be regarded as part of the mother, but this definition of murder appears to be sound. Application:** The House of Lords held that a child was not a live person and therefore this could not be murder.

CAUSATION: CAUSING DEATH

The killing must cause the death of a person. What needs to be proved is that the acts or omissions of the Defendant caused the death of the victim. Technically, "causing death", can be misconstrued because everyone will eventually die. The courts have acknowledged the fact, and consider it equally liable to cause death.

There are two important things to establish causation, both of which have to be proved by the prosecution. Firstly, the jury must be satisfied that the acts of omissions in question resulted in the relevant consequence. Secondly, it must be proved that the acts or omissions of the accused were a legal cause of the consequence.

General Principle: There must be a causal link between the act or omission and the death of the victim

Attorney-General's Reference (No.3 of 1994) [1997] 3 All ER 936, HL

Facts: A man was charged with stabbing his pregnant girlfriend in the abdomen while she was pregnant. This led to her giving birth prematurely, and the baby died some four months later as a result of its immaturity. **Ratio: The House of Lords said that the man could not be guilty of murder because he did not have the necessary *mens rea* towards the death of B, but had no doubt the *actus reus* of murder. The man's act changed the maternal environment of the foetus, said Lord Mustill, so that when the baby was born she died (albeit of "natural causes" and not of a minor injury sustained during the stabbing) when she would otherwise have lived. Lord Hope agreed, and said the *Actus Reus* of murder and manslaughter required evidence of an unbroken chain of causation between the defendant's act and the victim's death, the time interval now being unimportant. The presumed facts of the reference certainly created a *prima facie* case to go to the jury. Application:** If the prosecution cannot prove a causal link between the Defendant's act and the victim's death, there can be no conviction for murder.

In deciding the issue of causation, the jury must apply the following legal principles:

- **FACTUAL CAUSATION: THE 'BUT FOR' TEST**

This is a question of fact. It must be proved that 'but for' the act or omission of the Defendant, the relevant consequence would not have happened the way that it did. Which means that in the absence of the defendant's act or omission would the defendant have died?

General Principle: A factual link must be established between the act or omission of the accused and the victim's death.

R v White [1910] 2 KB 124, CCA
Facts: Meaning to kill his mother, the accused put a few drops of cyanide into her lemonade. Soon afterwards, before drinking the lemonade, his mother died of a heart attack. **Ratio: According to the 'but for' test, it must be established that the consequence would not have occurred as and when it did but for the Defendant's action. Application:** Since the medical evidence showed that the death of the mother was not due to poisoning and no trace of cyanide was found in the body the court acquitted the Defendant on the murder charge.

- **LEGAL CAUSATION**

This is a question of law. Quite generally a question becomes one of law where there is more than one operative cause. If I invite you around for dinner and throw a TV out the window as you ring the door bell and you are thrown into the road, hit by a cyclist who throws you into the way of and oncoming car and if you die. Who is the cause of death? The law will prevent a person from being responsible for everything that arises from his acts or omissions. The law will acknowledge the liability of the Defendant before imposing any penalty.

General Principle: The consequence must be caused by the Defendant's culpable act.

R v Dalloway (1847) 2 Cox CC
Facts: The Defendant was driving a horse cart without holding the reins. A child ran in front of the cart and was struck by the wheels and killed. It appeared in evidence that even if the Defendant would have been holding the reins, the child would have still been killed as he would not have been able to stop the cart in time. However, if he would not have been driving the cart then the child would not have been killed so in that way he did "cause death". **Ratio: The issue for the court was to establish whether the consequence could be said to be the result of the Defendant not holding the reins. Application:** Evidence shew

that even if the Defendant had been holding the reins, he could not have stopped the cart in time. Therefore, the Defendant was held not liable. The child's death was not the Defendant's fault.

General Principle: The defendant's act need not be the only cause of death.

R v Benge (1865) 4 F & F 504
Facts: Benge was a foreman of some railway track layers. He was under the impression that the next train was not due for a few hours and so he ordered the track to be taken up. He asked a man to go down the track with a red flag to stop any trains. However, this man did not go an appropriate distance and the driver of the train was not keeping a good look out. The train crashed and many people died as a consequence. **Ratio: The issue for the court was that the deaths were a combination of elements: The Defendant's misreading the train timetable, the signalman's failure to stand in the appropriate position, the train's driver's failure to keep a proper lookout. Before a situation of multiple causes, the court focused on which one of them was the major cause of the crash. Application:** The jury convicted the Defendant on the ground that his conduct mainly caused the deaths.

MURDER AND CAUSATION

General Principle: To convict D of murder, the prosecution must show that the drink was given to the subject with the plan to kill, that the drink was a (more than minimal) cause of death, and that V's act of drinking was not a free, willing, and informed choice that would have broken the chain of causation.

R v Field [2021] EWCA Crim 380

Facts: The defendant, D, was a young man who attempted to financially exploit an elderly man, V, by beguiling him. While posing as V's close friend, he influenced him to alter his will in favour of D by supplying him with alcohol and illegal substances over an extended period of time. Once this was accomplished, he carried out his plan to murder V by offering him sleeping pills and an entire bottle of liquor, which he knew V would be compelled to drink. V did so and perished of severe alcohol toxicity as a result.

Ratio: The judge instructed the jury that in order to convict D of murder, they must prove that the drink was given to the victim with the intent to kill, that the drink was a (more than minimal) cause of death, and that V's act of drinking was not a free, voluntary, and informed decision that would have broken the chain of causation. The court's primary concern was with causation. If V's consumption of alcohol and narcotics was voluntary, free, and informed, then causation was not established under the Kennedy (No. 2) principle, and the murder charge would be dismissed. Although the victim voluntarily consumed the alcohol and/or medication, the judge instructed the jury that D could still be culpable of homicide. In essence; he lacked an informed understanding of the "truly dangerous nature of the situation." In agreement with this analysis, the Court of Appeals upheld the conviction.
Application: In contrast to the Kennedy case, the victim in this instance was not fully aware of the consequences of injecting the substance. Rather, this victim was deceived into believing he was in secure hands with a person who loved him, when in reality he was being lured into a dangerous situation with a murderer.

INTERVENING ACTS OR ACTS WHICH BREAK THE LINK OF CAUSATION.

This is where the act of a third party breaks the causal effect of the original Defendant. The courts have to decide whether the link of causation has been broken and can the Defendant be held liable in such situations.

General Principle: Courts are reluctant to consider medical negligence as breaking the chain of causation.

R v Smith [1959] 2 All ER 193, CMAC

Facts: Smith and Creed were involved in a fight in barracks, in which Smith stabbed Creed with his bayonet. Creed's friend took him to the first aid post, but on the way he tripped over and dropped Creed twice. When they got there, the medical officer was busy and took some time to get to Creed. Creed died about two hours after the stabbing, but had he been given proper treatment he would probably have recovered. Smith was charged with murder. **Ratio: The treatment he was given was thoroughly bad and might well have affected his chances of recovery, said Lord Parker CJ, but medical treatment, correct or not, did not break the chain of causation. If at the time of death, the original wound is still an operating cause and a substantial cause: then death can be said to be a result of the wound albeit that some other cause is also operating. Only when the second cause of death is so overwhelming as to make the original wound merely part of the history can it be said that death does not flow from the wound. Application:** Generally, medical malpractice does not break the chain of causation. Therefore, the Defendant was not convicted.

General Principle: Bad medical treatment does not break the link of causation.

R v Cheshire [1991] 3 All ER 670, CA

Facts: The Defendant shot the victim in an argument, and the victim was taken to hospital where a tracheotomy was performed. Six weeks later, the victim suffered breathing problems as a result of the tracheotomy scar and died. The hospital had been negligent - perhaps even reckless - in not recognising the likely cause of the victim's problems and responding to them. **Ratio: The Defendant's actions need not be the sole or even the main cause of death as long as they contributed significantly to that result. Medical negligence does not exclude the Defendant's liability unless it was so independent of his acts and so potent as to make his own contribution insignificant. Application:** Only in the most extraordinary and unusual case would treatment, whether right or wrong, given in good faith by a generally competent doctor, be regarded as independent of the original injury. The Court of Appeal held that this did not break the chain of causation from the shooting.

- **INTERVENTION OF THIRD PARTIES**

General Principle: There will be a break in the chain of causation only if the acts of the third party are free and informed.

R v Pagett (1983) 76 Cr App R 279, CA
Facts: Pagett was convicted of manslaughter following the death of his pregnant girlfriend that had been hit and killed by police bullets while Pagett was using her as a human shield. **Ratio: The judge while directing the jurors on causation opined that they had to be sure that the accused had first fired at the police officers and that act caused the officers to fire back, which resulted in the girl being killed. The jury had to be satisfied that the police officers fired in self-defence or while performing their duties as a police officer. If the jury was not sure about these two then the link of causation would be broken. The jury convicted Pagett. The decision was appealed. The Court of Appeal said Pagett's act was not only a factual cause of Gail's death but a legal cause too: it was an unlawful and dangerous act, and the police return of fire was a foreseeable consequence.**
Application: There will only be a break in the chain of causation if the actions of the third party were 'free, deliberate and informed'.

- **NEW ACTS INTERVENING (NOVUS ACTUS INTERVENIENS)**

R v. Grant (Tony Lee) [2021] EWCA Crim 1243
Facts: The defendant, A, was the occupant in the front seat of a vehicle piloted by B. While seeking for two specific victims to attack with weapons, B, upon locating the men crossing the road, intentionally veered into them and killed them. A argued at trial that B's decision to run down the victims instead of waiting to attack one or both of them on foot in a face-to-face confrontation was such a departure from the agreed-upon plan that it constituted

an overwhelming supervening act (*novus actus interveniens*), rendering A guilty of manslaughter as opposed to murder. The judge disagreed and refused to submit the issue to the jury's decision. **Ratio: The Court of Appeal dismissed A's appeal, holding, among other things, that the central issue was whether Grant's conduct was** *"so distanced in time place or circumstances from the conduct of the perpetrator that it would not be realistic to regard his or her offence as encouraged or assisted by it"* (**R v Jogee** [2016] UKSC 8; 2017 AC 387). Not the case in this instance.

- ## THE 'THIN- SKULL' RULE

The Thin-skull rule refers to the principle that the Defendant must take the victim as he finds him. This means if my victim is prone to internal bleeding and I hurt them unknowingly, I am still responsible for their injuries.

General Principle: A person who inflicts harm on another cannot simply escape liability if the victim due to some pre-existing infirmity suffers greater harm than would be expected as a result of his act. In other words, the defendant must be taken as he/she has been found.

R v Hayward (1908) 21 Cox CC 692
Facts: The Defendant threatened his wife with violence and chased her out of the house, where she died from a rare medical condition aggravated by violent exercise and fright. Both Defendant and wife were unaware of the medical condition. **Ratio: The issues for the court were: firstly, whether the Defendant was liable even if he did not physically touch her. Secondly, should the peculiar medical condition of the victim have been taken into account. An ordinary person of reasonable fortitude would not have died in the same circumstances. Application:** Ridley J told the jury that death from fright alone, caused by an illegal act such as a threat of violence, was enough to sustain a charge of manslaughter. The Defendant had to take the victim's condition as he found it. The Defendant could not escape liability on the grounds that the death was caused by a medical condition.

• **ACTS OF THE VICTIM**

This issue generally arises in fright and flight cases. The issue falls on the question whether such escape was foreseeable by a reasonable man, if not then the Defendant can be acquitted.

General Principle: There must be some proportionality between the gravity of the threat and the action of the deceased in seeking to escape from it.

R v Mackie (1973) 57 Cr App R 453, CA
Facts: The Defendant threatened his three-year-old stepson with a severe thrashing for some minor misbehaviour. The boy tried to run away but fell downstairs, dislocated his neck and died. The Defendant was charged with manslaughter. The man was convicted and his conviction was upheld by the Court of Appeal.
Ratio: The judge had put four questions to the jury: Was the boy in fear of the Defendant? Did that fear cause him to try to escape? Was that fear well-founded? Was it caused by the Defendant's unlawful conduct, allowing for the fact that Defendant was in loco parentis and could lawfully administer reasonable punishment? These were the right questions and the jury had evidently answered each of them affirmatively.
Application: The defence that the boy had effectively killed himself by running and falling down the stairs was not accepted by the Court.

General Principle: If the victim has bled to death from the original wound, his act or omission done to commit suicide will not break the chain of causation.

R v Dear [1996] Crim LR 595, CA
Facts: A man attacked another man who had allegedly molested the defendant's 12-year-old daughter, cutting him repeatedly and deeply with a Stanley knife. The victim died two days later and the defendant was charged with murder. On appeal, the defendant argued that the victim had in fact committed suicide by reopening his healing wounds, or alternatively by failing to stem the bleeding from them after they had reopened themselves. **Ratio: The Court**

of Appeal said if the victim mistreats or neglects to treat his
injuries, this would not break the chain of causation.**
Application: The jury was directed in considering the Defendant
liable since the victim's wounds were still the operating and
substantial cause of the death. The defence that the chain of
causation got broken due to suicide or failure to take steps to
staunch the blood flow were not available.

- ## REFUSAL OF MEDICAL TREATMENT

In these cases, the courts have to decide the position when the
victim refuses medical treatment.

**General Principle: Even if the victim refuses medical
treatment, the Defendant will be liable for causing the death
of the victim.**

R v Holland (1841) 174 ER 313

Facts: The Defendant assaulted the victim and injured one of his fingers. A surgeon advised the victim to have the finger amputated to prevent infection. The victim refused and subsequently died of tetanus. **Ratio: The Defendant was held to have caused the death of the victim. The fact that the wound did not instantly cause death and became a cause of death after the victim refused treatment did not matter. The issue that only needed to be established was whether the wound was the cause of the death. Application:** Refusal of medical treatment by the victim could not be used a defence for murder. The Defendant was held liable.

General Principle: The Defendant cannot escape liability on the grounds that the victim had refused treatment on religious grounds.

R v Blaue [1975] 3 All ER 446, CA

Facts: The Defendant stabbed a 18-year-old woman and punctured her lung. At the hospital, the woman was told that she would have needed a blood transfusion to save her life, but she refused this as contrary to her religious beliefs. She died next day. The Defendant was charged with murder which was subsequently reduced to manslaughter by reason of diminished responsibility. **Ratio: It has long been the policy of the law, said Lawton LJ that those who use violence on other people must take their victims as they find them. This principle clearly applies to the mental as well as the physical characteristics of the victim, and the courts will rarely make a judgement as to whether the victim's response was reasonable. Application:** The Defendant could not escape liability because the victim had refused treatment on religious grounds.

SUMMARY

- Homicide means causing the death of another human being.

- Murder is the most serious kind of homicide. The Defendant must not only kill someone but he must act with a specific intent.

- The element of Actus Reus of murder is satisfied whether the killing is unlawful.

- There must be a link between the action of the Defendant and the death of the victim. It must be established that the consequence would not have occurred as and when it did but for the Defendant's action.

- The courts have to decide whether the link of causation has been broken by considering acts of third parties, the thin-skull rule and acts of the victim.

Chapter 3 - Mens Rea

INTRODUCTION

The *mens rea* is the mental element of crime. It is the guilty intention to bring about a desired result which is considered criminal. The mens rea of murder is conventionally explained as "malice aforethought", but this can be deceptive because (as Lord Hailsham LC pointed out) neither word takes its usual meaning. Malice needs not be truly malicious - euthanasia for reasons of compassion is still murder - and no more than a split second's premeditation is necessary. Moreover, murder can be committed without the intention to cause death: the *mens rea* is an intention to cause either death or grievous bodily harm to any person.

The Homicide Act of 1957 explains *mens rea* for murder, 'malice afterthought' as:

1) An intention to kill (express malice) or

2) An intention to cause grave bodily harm (implied malice)

DIRECT INTENTION

There are two kinds of intention in criminal law: direct intention and oblique intention. Direct intention is where the consequence is what the Defendant wanted to happen by his act, it was the purpose of the Defendant's act.

General Principle: The intention will be direct whether the Defendant desires an outcome.

R v Calhaem [1985] 1 QB 808

Facts: The Defendant hired a killer to murder a woman. The killer testified that after being paid by the Defendant he had decided not to carry out the killing, but instead to visit the victim's house, carrying an unloaded shotgun and a hammer, to act out a charade that would give the appearance that he had tried to kill her. When he had stepped inside the front door of the woman's house, she started screaming. He panicked, hitting her several times with the hammer. The Defendant appealed, submitting that there was no causal connection between him and the death of the woman. **Ratio: Hiring someone to kill carries a direct intention of a specific outcome which is murder a person. Application:** The Court of Appeal affirmed the Defendant's conviction on the ground that by hiring the killer he had the *actus reus* and direct *mens rea* required for being guilty of murder.

General Principle: It is the jury's task to decide on the matter of intention.

R v Moloney [1985] 1 All ER 1025, HL

Facts: The Defendant and his stepfather, who had been drinking, got into an argument as to which could load and fire a shotgun more quickly. They decided to test their respective claims by practical experiment, in the course of which the Defendant shot his stepfather in the face at a range of about six feet, killing him instantly. The defendant claimed that he had not deliberately aimed the gun, and had simply pulled the trigger in response to the victim's taunts, but the jury found him guilty of murder. **Ratio: The House of Lords were highly critical of a statement in Archbold that a man intends the consequence of his action when he foresees that it will probably happen. Lord Bridge suggested that where a special direction was necessary the jury might be invited to consider (i) whether death or serious injury was a "natural consequence" of the Defendant's actions, and (ii) whether the Defendant foresaw that consequence and to infer the appropriate intention if and only if they could answer yes to both questions. Application:** Although it has since been suggested that it may sometimes be necessary to give a jury an elaborated direction on the meaning of intention in rare cases where the Defendant does an act which is manifestly dangerous, and as a result someone dies, but where the primary desire or motive may not have been to harm that person.

OBLIQUE INTENTION

Oblique intention refers to those circumstances where the Defendant does not necessarily desire an outcome but he appreciates as inevitable the side effect of his action. He will be considered to have an intention to commit the *actus reus* even if he has oblique intent.

The Draft Criminal Code includes oblique intention in the definition of intention:

According to Section 1 'a person acts

(a) 'intentionally' with respect to a result when –

(i) it is his purpose to cause it, or

(ii) although it is not his purpose to cause it, he knows that it would occur in the ordinary course of events if he were to succeed in his purpose of casing some other result

General Principle: The foresight of virtual certainty can be used as an evidence of intention.

Hyam v DPP [1974] 2 All ER 41, HL

Facts: The Defendant, who was a man's lover, became suspicious of his relationship with another woman. She went to the other woman's house, poured petrol through the letter-box, and lit it, causing a serious fire. The woman's two daughters died in the fire, and the Defendant was charged with their murder. Her defence was that she intended only to frighten the woman into breaking off her relationship with her lover and that he had not intended to kill anyone. **Ratio: Lord Hailsham LC said it was sufficient for murder that the Defendant knew there was a serious risk of death or grievous bodily harm and went on to commit the acts with the intention of exposing a potential victim to such a risk. Lords Diplock and Kilbrandon dissented as to the sufficiency of grievous bodily harm, but all agreed that foresight was as good as intention. Application:** The House of Lords by a majority dismissed the Defendant's appeal against conviction. This decision flew in the face of Section 8 of the Criminal Justice Act 1967 and is now generally regarded as having been wrongly decided.

General Principle: It is for the jury to decide that what degree of foresight is required for an inference of intention.

R v Hancock & Shankland [1986] 1 All ER 641, HL

Facts: During the coal miners' strike, two striking miners decided they would try to stop non-strikers from getting to work. They stood on a bridge over the motorway and when they saw a taxi approaching in which a blackleg was travelling, they pushed over a lump of concrete meaning for it to land on the road in front of the taxi. In fact, the concrete hit the taxi itself and killed the taxi-driver, and the two miners were charged with murder. **Ratio: The greater the probability of a consequence, the more likely it is that it was foreseen. If it was foreseen, the more likely it is that it was intended. But it is entirely up to the jury to decide what degree of foresight is required for an inference of intention and no simple formula can replace the jury's right and duty to make its own decision. Application:** The Defendants could have easily foreseen that their act could lead to these consequences. Therefore, his conviction was confirmed.

General Principle: The necessary intention can be inferred when death or serious bodily harm was a virtual certainty.

R v Nedrick [1986] 3 All ER 1, CA

Facts: The Defendant set fire to a house belonging to a woman against whom he had a grudge. The woman's child died in the fire. **Ratio: The trial judge (before the judgements in Moloney and Hancock & Shankland had been published) directed the jury as to intention in a way that was now clearly inappropriate, and the Court of Appeal quashed the defendant's conviction for murder and substituted manslaughter. Where the charge is murder, said Lord Lane CJ, and in the rare cases where a simple direction as to intention is not enough, the jury should be directed that they are not entitled to infer the necessary intention unless they feel sure that death or serious bodily harm was a virtual certainty - barring some unforeseen intervention - as a result of the Defendant's actions, and that the defendant realised such was the case. Where a man realises**

that it is for all practical purposes inevitable that his actions will result in death or serious harm, the inference might be irresistible that he intends that result, however little he might desire or wish it to happen. The decision is one for the jury to be reached on a consideration of all the evidence. Application:** The Court of Appeal held that there was a clear misdirection of the jury by the judge. The directions illustrated are the ones the jury should have followed.

General Principle: The jury is not entitled to find the necessary intention unless death or serious bodily harm was an obvious conclusion to the defendant's act.

R v Woollin [1998] 4 All ER 103, HL

Facts: A man lost his temper with his three-month-old son and threw the child onto a hard surface, causing head injuries from which the child died. The Defendant was charged with murder and the judge directed the jury, largely in accordance with the Nedrick guidelines, that they might infer the necessary intention if they were satisfied that the Defendant realised there was "a substantial risk" of serious injury. **Ratio: The House of Lords said this would enlarge the scope of murder and blur the distinction between that and manslaughter. The jury, said Lord Steyn, should be directed that they are not entitled to find the necessary intention unless they feel sure that death or serious bodily harm was a virtual certainty - barring some unforeseen intervention - as a result of the defendant's actions, and that the defendant realised such was the case, but should be reminded that the decision is one for them on a consideration of all the evidence. Application:** The House of Lords accepted the appeal of the Defendant. The Courts, by leaving the direction on oblique intention in the negative and thus giving juries some leeway to avoid convicting, have allowed juries to make moral judgments in appropriate circumstances.

MOTIVE AND INTENTION

Intention must not be confused with motive or desire. Even though the defendant has a motive (for example, a reason to kill) that does not mean that when he commits the *actus reus* he can be automatically be taken to have the intention to kill.

General Principle: Motive is not same as intention.

Chandler v DPP [1964] AC 763

Facts: The Appellants were against nuclear weapons and planned a non-violent action to immobilise an aircraft at a RAF station for six hours. They were convicted of conspiracy under section 1 of the Official Secrets Act 1911 since they entered 'a prohibited place for a purpose which is prejudicial to the safety or interests of the state'. **Ratio: If a person enters a prohibited place in order to cause obstruction and interference which is prejudicial to the defence dispositions of the state, an offence is committed. The Defendant cannot claim that his ultimate purpose was not to commit the offence. Application:** The judge held that where the jury was satisfied that the appellant's immediate purpose was proven, it was right to find the appellant's guilty. Their motive behind their action was irrelevant as they still intended the method of achieving it.

RECKLESSNESS

The Defendant takes an unjustified risk that might cause a serious consequence with awareness of that risk.

General Principle: It is necessary to establish that the Defendant took an unjustifiable risk to establish recklessness as clarified in the following case.

Cunningham [1957] 2 QB 396 (CA)

Facts: Cunningham was convicted of unlawfully and maliciously causing the victim to take a noxious thing which endangered her life, contrary to section 23 of the Offences Against the Person Act 1861. **Ratio: It was held that the term ''maliciously' in an offence assumes foresight of the consequence. Hence, while dealing with offences involving 'malice' it is not enough that**

the risk would have been obvious to the Defendant if he had reconsidered his decision. He must know the existence of 'risk' and must consciously take it. The prosecution will have to prove that the Defendant had a particular state of mind while committing the offence as opposed to considering the state of mind of any reasonable person. Application:** An actual intention to cause the kind of harm that was done is important. The Defendant was convicted.

General Principle: The Defendant may escape liability if he was subjectively unaware of the risks.

R v G and Another [2003] UKHL 50

Facts: Two boys, aged 11 and 12 went to the back yard of a shop and lit some newspapers and threw them under a wheelie bin. The burning papers set fire to the shop which spread to the eaves of building which consequently caused the roof to fall, amounting to £1million worth of damage. The boys were charged with reckless arson to the building contrary to Section 1(3) of the Criminal Damage Act 1971. **Ratio: The House of Lords held that** *subjective* **recklessness (defined in** *Cunningham*) **should apply to criminal damage. Lord Bingham referred to the definition of recklessness laid down in Clause 18 of the Law Commissions Draft Criminal Code (1989):**

A person acts recklessly within the meaning of Section 1 of the Criminal Damage Act 1971 with respect to –

i) a circumstance when he is aware of a risk that it exists or will exist;

ii) a result when he is aware of a risk that it will occur;

and it is, in the circumstances known to him, unreasonable to take that risk.

Application: Hence, since the boys were subjectively unaware of the risk their convictions were quashed. The House of Lords established that the legal test of recklessness coming from Cunningham and *R v G* was the same but they referred to different crimes. The test from *R v G* covers cases relating to criminal damage and the Cunningham test is applicable to all the other scenarios. The test from *R v G* overturns and confines **Caldwell** recklessness to the history books.

TRANSFERRED MALICE

Whether the Defendant has the *mens rea* of a particular crime and he acts causing the actus reus of that crime, he cannot say that the *actus reus* was carried out in a way that was not exactly as he intended it.

General Principle: An intention to kill one person can be transferred to another if the second is the one who actually dies from the Defendant's act.

R v Mitchell [1983] 2 All ER 427

Facts: The Defendant and another man became involved in a scuffle in a Post Office. The Defendant pushed the other man, who fell onto an elderly lady, causing her injuries from which she later died. **Ratio: The Court of Appeal upheld the Defendant's conviction for manslaughter as his intention to assault the man was transferred to the elderly lady, the victim. Application:** The Court saw no reason to hold that an act calculated to harm someone could not be transferred to manslaughter on that person that was actually killed by the action of the Defendant.

General Principle: If two people are engaged in serious conflict and in the process one kills an uninvolved person, the other engaged party would be treated as in a joint enterprise with the killer. Coupled with transferred malice, when one of the parties kills another, his malice transfers, and so to is the other combatant guilty of the murder (by being in conflict with the person who killed another while trying to kill you.)

R v Gnango [2011] UKSC 59

Facts: The defendant was a teenager engaged in gang warfare, and had been in conflict with another person known as TC, took a gun and went to look for him. While out searching in a car park, the defendant came under fire from a person known as "Bandana Man" (suspected to be TC). The defendant returned fire. a 26 woman crossing the car park was shot by a BM, and died. BM was not apprehended and nor was TC (if they were different people).

The defendant was charged with murder under the joint enterprise rules. The issue was whether the defendant could be guilty of murder, through a join between the principles of joint enterprise and transferred malice **Ratio: The law on joint enterprise could treat two defendants as acting together, even if they were only engaged in attempting to harm or kill one other. Therefore, if one kills another while attempting to kill his target, as his malice/intention will be transferred toward the victim, thus whoever he is in joint enterprise with is also guilty.** Application: Therefore, as BM intended to kill the defendant, his malice is transferred when he kills the victim, and because the defendant was in conflict with BM, he was in joint enterprise and hence inherited BM's liability. The defendant was guilty.

CO- INCIDENCE OF *ACTUS REUS* AND *MENS REA*

The *actus reus* and the *mens rea* must normally coincide in time, but the courts are prepared to take a broad view.

General Principle: The requirement that the *actus reus* and *mens rea* must go together may be interpreted by the court in the light of the facts of the case.

R v Thabo Meli and others [1954] 1 All ER 373

Facts: The Defendants took the victim to a hut. They beat him. Believing him to be dead, they threw his body over a cliff in the attempts to make it look as an accident. The victim was still alive when thrown and he died afterwards from exposure. The Defendants tried to argue that the actus reus on which the death for exposure was based was separated in time from the *mens rea.* **Ratio: The court pointed out that it is not possible to divide up what is one series of acts. Application:** The court convicted the Defendants on the ground that all their acts were set out to achieve a specific plan. The fact that their purpose was achieved before the actual death of the victim did not separate the two elements of *actus reus* and *mens rea.*

General Principle: In case of a continuing act, it is enough that the Defendant had *mens rea* at some point during the act. This is known as the 'continuing act theory'.

Fagan v Metropolitan Police Commissioner [1969] 1QB 439

Facts: Fagan drove on a policeman's foot accidentally. When asked to move off his foot by the policeman, Fagan refused to comply. He was charged with assaulting a police officer in the execution of his duty. At the time of driving on the foot, which was *actus reus* of the crime he did not have *mens rea*. **Ratio: Whether an action of the Defendant is not at first criminal since the Defendant has no *mens rea*, but it becomes criminal when the Defendant intentionally decides to carry out the action, the exact coincidence between the two elements become irrelevant. Application:** Even though the defendant did not have the *mens rea* at the beginning of his unlawful action, he had it at some point during the act. Therefore, the Defendant was convicted since he intentionally left the wheel on the officer's foot.

THE TRANSACTION PRINCIPLE

General Principle: The courts sometimes categorise the series of acts of the Defendant into a transaction and it is enough to establish that the Defendant has *mens rea* at some point during this transaction.

R v Thabo Meli and others [1954] 1 All ER 373, PC (South Africa)

Facts: Thabo Meli and his friends took their victim to a small hut and beat him over the head intending to kill him. Thinking they had succeeded, they rolled his body over a cliff to make the death appear accidental. In fact, the victim survived both the beating and the rolling, but died from exposure shortly afterwards. Meli and the others were convicted of murder. **Ratio: The Privy Council, dismissing their appeal, said that where the actus reus consists of a series of linked acts, it is enough that the mens rea existed at some time during that series, even if not necessarily at the time of the particular act which caused the death. Application:** The fact that *mens rea* existed at some point during the transaction was enough to uphold their conviction.

CAUSATION

The two elements of *actus reus* and *mens rea* can be looked at in terms of causation. A link between the two may be considered sufficient whether they cooperate in reaching the outcome.

General Principle: The problem of co-incidence of *actus reus* and *mens rea* can be overlooked by considering the act done with the *mens rea* (the first act) as causing the subsequent acts.

R v Masilela (1968) (2) SA 558

Facts: The Defendants hit the victim over his head, left him on his bed and then set the house on fire. Evidence showed that the death of the victim was caused by the fire. **Ratio: The judge held that the earlier acts of Defendants which were committed with the *mens rea* of murder were the cause of the death because if the victim had not been unconscious he would not have stayed in the house. Application:** The Defendants' earlier acts of beating were done with *mens rea* of murder and were the actual cause of death.

MISTAKE

There are circumstances in which the court may take into consideration a mistaken consideration of the Defendant. Nevertheless, the defence of ignorance of the law does not allow the escape from liability.

General Principle: The type of mistake will determine the effect on the Defendant's liability when he commits a mistake.

IGNORANCE OF LAW

General Principle: The Defendant's ignorance of the law does not absolve him of his liability. Hence, the saying, 'ignorance of law is no excuse'.

R v Lee [2000] EWCA Crim 53

Facts: The defendant had failed a breath test. He looked at the test result and saw an air bubble which pushed the test over the limit.

When the officer tried to arrest him for drink driving the defendant punched him. He was convicted of assaulting a police officer with intent to resist arrest under s.38 Offence against the Person Act 1861. He contended that he genuinely believed that the arrest was unlawful. **Ratio: If the mistake was one of the law, the defence will not apply. Application:** As the mistake was one of law, the defendant was found guilty.

MISTAKES THAT NEGATE THE *MENS REA*

General Principle: A mistake of some element of the *actus reus* can prevent the Defendant from having the required mens *rea*.

R v Smith [1974] 1 All ER 632

Facts: A tenant with his landlord's consent, installed in his flat some electrical wiring for stereo equipment and covered it over with ceiling and wall panels and floor boards. When he surrendered his lease, he tore away the panels (which as a matter of land law had now become the landlord's property) to remove the wiring and was charged with criminal damage. **Ratio: Allowing his appeal and quashing his conviction, the Court of Appeal declined to apply Section 5(2)(a) of the Criminal Damage Act 1961, but said that where the Defendant honestly believed the property was his own he lacked the necessary *mens rea* with regard to the circumstances. Application:** The Defendant did not recklessly or intentionally damage property belonging to the other as required by the Criminal Damage Act.

SUMMARY

- The concept of *mens rea* refers to the mind of the person committing the unlawful action.

- *Mens rea* may constitute intention, recklessness, malice, negligence and dishonesty.

- Intention is the highest form of *mens rea* essential in order to establish murder.

- Recklessness is the form of *mens rea* used in non-fatal offences against persons.

- 'Transferred malice' is a principle that refers to those circumstances where the Defendant has actus reus and mens rea but the way he carried out the actus reus was not exactly as he planned.

- The elements of actus reus and mens rea must coincide at some point in time.

- The court might take into consideration in some specific circumstances whether the Defendant has mistakenly acted.

Chapter 4 - Omissions

INTRODUCTION

This chapter will discuss circumstances in which an accused will be liable by omission for an offence requiring *mens rea.*

A LEGAL DUTY TO ACT

There are certain situations where a duty to act exists:

- **A SPECIAL RELATIONSHIP**

Examples of these special relationships are: parents and their children, doctors and patients and attorneys and their clients. A parent is clearly under a duty of care to care for his child or children.

General Principle: Where there is duty to act, failure to do so can lead to criminal liability.

R v Gibbins & Proctor (1918) 13 Cr App R 134
Facts: The Defendant and his mistress were convicted of the murder of his seven-year-old daughter Nelly. They had starved the child to death and the jury found this to have been their intention (though the woman, who hated Nelly, was clearly the moving force). **Ratio: Where a duty to act is established due to the particular relationship between the parties, failure to do so can lead to criminal liability even for murder if the necessary** *mens rea* **is present. Application:** A parent is clearly under a duty to care for his or her children. The Defendants were both convicted.

General Principle: The parents are under a legal duty to protect their children.

Re A (Children) [2000] 4 All ER 961
Facts: This was the "Siamese twins case" where Jodie and Mary were joined in such a way that Jodie's heart and lungs were providing oxygenated blood for both. Medical opinion broadly

agreed that both would die in three to six months - or possibly slightly more - if nothing was done. Doctors sought the leave of the court to separate the twins, giving Jodie a good chance of a fairly "normal" life, but causing the immediate death of Mary. The twins' parents opposed the application for religious reasons. **Ratio: In the Court of Appeal, Brooke LJ said there could be no doubt that in English law, a surgeon who performed the separation knowing that it would inevitably hasten Mary's death would be held to have caused that death and to have done so intentionally, even though that would not have been his primary motive. So far as the law was concerned, the doctrine of double effect did not apply here because Mary's death would not be a side-effect of treatment that was in her best interests overall. Application:** The judge observed that it was the legal duty of the parents to save the twin that could be saved.

• VOLUNTARY ASSUMPTION OF DUTY OF CARE

If a person voluntarily assumes a duty towards another person, then the law will hold him responsible in the event of his failure to carry out the duty.

General Principle: Duty of care can be extended to unrelated persons who voluntarily undertake responsibility.

R v Stone & Dobinson [1977] 2 All ER 341
Facts: Stone lived with his mistress Dobinson. They both accepted Stone's elderly sister to live with them; when she became incapable of looking after herself they neglected to care for her and she died. **Ratio: On the evidence, the jury were entitled to find as a matter of fact that even though they were under no legal duty, the two of them had taken on themselves the duty of caring for the elderly sister, and that they had failed in that duty. The issue of whether a duty of care arises will always be determined by the facts of the case. Application:** The Defendants were convicted of manslaughter.

CONTRACTUAL DUTIES

Whether the failure to perform a contract may endanger lives, the law imposes a duty to act.

General Principle: A duty can be owed by the Defendant to a party he has entered into a contract with or to a third party.

R v Pittwood (1902) 19 TLR 37
Facts: The Defendant was a level crossing keeper who negligently left open the crossing gate. This led to the death of a carter whose cart was struck by a train. **Ratio: He was convicted of manslaughter. He had a duty (arising from his contract of employment) to shut the gate and although this duty was owed to his employers rather than to the public at large, it was enough that his negligent failure to act could lead to conviction. Application:** His failure to close the gate could amount to *actus reus* of manslaughter by omission because he was under a contractual duty to close the gate when the train was approaching.

WHEN THE ACCUSED CREATES A DANGEROUS SITUATION

Whether the Defendant by accident and without the *mens rea* required does something that endanger lives, as soon as he is aware of it, he has a duty to take all steps required to prevent or reduce the danger.

General Principle: When the accused has created a dangerous situation he is under the duty to prevent the damage.

R v Miller [1983] 1 All ER 978, HL
Facts: A squatter took shelter in an empty house and went to sleep with a cigarette in his hand. He awoke a little later to find that he had set the mattress alight. He got up, went into another room and went to sleep there. The fire took hold and the house burned down. **Ratio: His conviction for arson was upheld by the House of Lords: having accidentally created the dangerous situation, he had a duty to take steps to remove the danger and his failure to do so was sufficient. If an individual sets in motion a chain of events that can cause damage and if the individual becomes**

aware of the damage and can prevent it, his omission to do so becomes *actus reus* of criminal damage. Application: The Defendant did not take measures to counteract a danger he had created himself which led to criminal liability.

WITHHOLDING LIFE SAVING TREATMENT

According to this principle a doctor has a general duty to act in the best interest of the patient, making all reasonable effort to keep the patient alive. Whether the patient's best interest requires the omission of the administration of lifesaving treatment, the law will consider it lawful.

General Principle: A doctor is under a duty to make reasonable efforts to keep a patient alive however, 'keep alive' is different from the duty of 'not to kill'.

R v Arthur [1985] Crim LR 705
Facts: A doctor, who was treating a Down's syndrome child noted that his parents did not wish for him to survive, ordered 'nursing care only' and the administration of a drug to stop the child seeking sustenance. **Ratio: This was one of the first cases in which the English criminal courts judicially recognised that it may be lawful to omit to administer lifesaving treatment, although the circumstances in which this would be the case were not fully examined. The court established a clear distinction between the duty to 'keep the patient alive' and the duty 'not to kill' him. Application:** The doctor was not held guilty of homicide even when the child starved to death.

General Principle: A doctor is under a duty to make reasonable efforts to keep a patient alive.

Airedale Health Authority v Bland [1993] 1 All ER 821
Facts: A young man was in a persistent vegetative state after being seriously injured at the Hillsborough football ground. Doctors sought leave from the court to discontinue artificial feeding so that he could "die with dignity". **Ratio: Lord Goff said that where a doctor gives lawful treatment (e.g. by administering drugs to relieve pain) the patient's subsequent death (as a side-effect, even if it was a very likely one) will be regarded in law as exclusively caused by the injury or disease. The law draws a crucial distinction between cases in which a doctor decides not to provide treatment which might prolong**

a patient's life and those in which he decides actively to bring the patient's life to an end. The former might be lawful if it was no longer in the patient's best interests (and thus no longer the doctors' duty) to keep him alive, but the latter never is. **Application:** It was lawful for Bland's doctors not to go on feeding him, intending him thereby to die. The court pointed out the major distinction between an act and an omission. 'Ending' and 'not continuing' were held to be two different things: one is deemed to be an act which cannot be justified and the latter is an omission, which may be.

SUMMARY

- The majority of criminal offences require the performance of an act.

- There are circumstances in which a person may be guilty because of omission to act.

- Whether the Defendant is under a legal duty to act, its failure may him guilty for criminal offence.

- The presence of a special relationship between the parties may arise a legal duty to act.

- Whether the Defendant acts in a way that makes assume his voluntary assumption of responsibility, the Defendant must act in conformity.

- The Defendant must comply with a contract whether its failure will endanger lives.

- The creation of a danger will require the Defendant to do his best to prevent endanger lives.

- A doctor is under a duty to act in the best interest of his patient.

Chapter 5 - Loss of Control & Diminished Responsibility

INTRODUCTION

This chapter will focus on the two defences which are available only for murder: loss of control and diminished responsibility.

LOSS OF CONTROL

The defence of provocation has been replaced by the defence of loss of control. The new defence is introduced by Section 54 of the Coroners and Justice Act 2009 and appears to retain the basic structure of the old law of provocation. The Defendant must have lost self-control as a result of something (a "qualifying trigger"). The jury must establish that a reasonable person, as the age and sex of the Defendant, might have reacted in the same way.

LOSS OF SELF CONTROL

This element is not clarified by the new Act but since it formed a necessary part of the old law it seems likely that it will continue to be an important element.

General Principle: The Defendant must have lost self-control at the time when the murder took place, as a consequence of the qualifying trigger.

R v Richens [1993] 4 All ER 877
Facts: The Defendant, who was 17, killed the man who raped his girlfriend. The deceased taunted him about the rape at which point he lost control and stabbed him. **Ratio: The Court held that this loss of control 'need not be a complete loss of control', so that the Defendant is not aware of what he is doing, merely 'a loss of control' where he was unable to restrain himself is enough.** **Application:** The question whether the Defendant actually lost control is for the jury to establish.

THE QUALIFYING TRIGGER

The "qualifying trigger" is defined under Section 55 of the Act as the cause of loss of control. There are two different qualifying triggers under this Section: 'a fear of serious violence' and a 'justifiable sense of being seriously wronged'.

FEAR OF SERIOUS VIOLENCE

General Principle: The actual trigger could be a combination of the two triggers.

R v Martin (Anthony) [2002] Crim LR 136
Facts: A farmer was convicted of murder and wounding with intent after shooting two burglars in his home. **Ratio: The jury apparently determined that in firing an (unlicensed) shotgun three times towards a torchlight he had intended to cause serious injury but not to kill, and had gone beyond the "reasonable force" that he could properly have used to defend himself and his property. Application:** Under the old law, it would have been a struggle to convince a jury that he had suddenly lost his self-control, given the degree of planning involved.

JUSTIFIABLE SENSE OF BEING SERIOUSLY WRONGED

In this case the trigger must come from something said or done and the Act states that this must amount to 'circumstances of an extremely grave character'.

General Principle: The trigger can be invoked by cumulative provocation that has been offered over a period of time.

R v Ahluwalia [1992] 4 All ER 889
Facts: A woman had entered into an "arranged marriage" and had been very badly treated by her husband. He had been violent and abusive towards her. He had threatened to kill her and had once tried to run her down. He had taunted her about his affair with another woman. One evening the Defendant poured petrol over

his bed as he slept and set light to it. She pleaded manslaughter claiming that she had not intended to kill him, just to cause him pain. She was convicted of murder and she appealed. **Ratio: The Court pointed out the presence of a qualifying trigger in the threat to kill expressed by the husband. The issue was whether the defence of provocation as 'sudden and temporary loss of control' might mitigate the sentence of murder. Since the Defendant's action did not immediately follow the husband's provocation, the Court talked about 'slow burn' reaction.** Application: Since the acts of the husband were the qualified trigger, the Court redirected the case to the jury pointing out the question of diminished responsibility due to the Defendant's depression developed after years of abuses.

General Principle: The trigger can be invoked by cumulative provocation offered over a period of several months.

R v Humphreys [1995] 4 All ER 1008
Facts: A woman of 17, working as a prostitute, stabbed and killed the 32-year old man with whom she was living. He had been violent towards her on several occasions and when she cut her wrists, apparently seeking attention rather than seriously attempting suicide, he taunted her with her incompetence. **Ratio: The Defendant was charged with murder and convicted. Allowing her appeal some ten years later, the Court of Appeal said the judge had erred in not clearly directing the jury's attention to the cumulative provocation offered over several months before the final taunt.** By 'cumulative provocation' the Court referred to their 'tempestuous relationship' that faced 'several distinct and cumulative strands of potentially provocative conduct building up until the final encounter'. This was the qualifying trigger. **Application:** The Court allowed the Defendant's appeal for conviction of murder. The jury had to take in consideration the cumulative provocation as qualifying trigger in order to replace the verdict with one of manslaughter.

LIMITATIONS ON THE USE OF THE DEFENCE

General Principle: This defence will not be available when the offence is an act of revenge.

R v Ibrams & Gregory [1981] 74 Cr App R 154
Facts: Two men and a woman had been bullied and terrorised by a person over a period up to and including a particular Sunday, and had been unable to obtain police protection. On Wednesday the three of them planned to beat up this person the following Sunday and break his arms and legs. This plan was duly carried out, and the man died of his injuries. **Ratio: Whether there are no, or insufficient, evidence of provocation of any loss of control, it is not reasonable to direct the jury in considering a qualifying trigger that does not exist as defence. Application:** The trial judge withdrew the defence of provocation from the jury, there having been no evidence of any provocative behaviour during the week or at the time of the man's death.

General Principle: It is no longer allowed to use this defence when the Defendant was the initial antagonist.

R v Johnson [1989] 2 All ER 839
 Facts: The Defendant made violent threats towards another man and his girlfriend. The man in turn grabbed the Defendant and pinned him against a wall, holding a glass in his other hand, but when the man let go of the glass the Defendant stabbed him fatally with a flick-knife. **Ratio: Whether there is evidence that the Defendant killed a person because he was provoked to do so, the defence of provocation should be left to the jury. Application:** The Court of Appeal substituted the verdict of murder in one of manslaughter. The trial judge erred in ruling that self-induced provocation could not be an available defence. Nevertheless, new law has overruled this case.

THE REASONABLE MAN TEST UNDER COMMON LAW

General Principle: The jury should then consider whether an ordinary person in the same circumstances would have been similarly provoked and would have reacted in a similar way.

Bedder v DPP [1954] 2 All ER 801

Facts: An 18-year-old Defendant went to a prostitute, but impotence made him unable to perform. The woman jeered at him, slapped him and kicked him in the groin, and he stabbed her. **Ratio: The case of *Bedder* is no longer regarded as good law. Recent cases seem to show that there is not just one reasonable person, but many, and the House of Lords have suggested that comparison should be with the "ordinary person" similar to the Defendant in every relevant way except for his state of intoxication and the shortness of his temper. Application:** The Defendant's plea of provocation was dismissed and he was convicted of murder. The House of Lords upheld the conviction by clarifying that the Defendant's reaction was to be compared with that of a reasonable man, and a reasonable man (not being impotent) would not have been so provoked.

THE REASONABLE MAN TEST UNDER THE HOMICIDE ACT 1957

General Principle: The objective test was broadened to take into account the age and sex of the defendant as well as characteristics that affected the gravity of the provocation.

DPP v Camplin [1978] 2 All ER 168

Facts: A boy of 15 went with a man in his fifties, who buggered him against his will and then taunted him; the boy responded by hitting the man over the head with a heavy pan, killing him. The boy was charged with murder and claimed he had been provoked. **Ratio: The "reasonable man" to be considered was an ordinary person of either sex, not exceptionally excitable or pugnacious, but possessed of such power of self-control as everyone was entitled to expect his fellow-citizens to exercise in today's society. Application:** Allowing his appeal against conviction, and substituting a verdict of manslaughter, the Court of Appeal distinguished Bedder on the grounds that impotence is an abnormal condition while age is not, and said the jury should have been directed to compare the Defendant's response with that of a reasonable 15-year-old. The House of Lords dismissed a further appeal by the Crown; since the Homicide Act 1957, said

Lord Diplock, Bedder was no longer relevant. This case expanded the objective test under Bedder.

General Principle: The Defendant's mental state was just as relevant as physical characteristics while considering the test

R v Ahluwalia [1992] 4 All ER 889
Facts: The Defendant entered into an "arranged marriage" and had been very badly treated by her husband. He had been violent and abusive towards her; he had threatened to kill her and had once tried to run her down; and he had taunted her about his affair with another woman. One evening the woman poured petrol over his bed as he slept and set light to it. She was charged with murder, and claimed provocation. **Ratio: The Court of Appeal began to adopt a more subjective approach by considering the Defendant's characteristics while evaluating the reaction of a reasonable man on a more general basis. Application:** The Court of Appeal said characteristics relating to the Defendant's mental state or personality, assuming they had the necessary degree of permanence, were just as relevant as physical ones, and that the jury might have been invited to consider not just the defendant's status as an Asian wife and her level of education but also (had any evidence to that effect been given at the trial) the probability that she was suffering from a condition known as "battered woman syndrome".

General Principle: Same standards of behaviour are expected of everyone, regardless of their individual psychological make-up.

R v Smith (Morgan) [2000] 4 All ER 289
Facts: A man killed another man in the course of an argument; he put forward a defence based on self-defence, diminished responsibility and provocation, but was convicted of murder. **Ratio: The Court of Appeal substituted a conviction for manslaughter, and said the judge had been wrong to tell the jury to ignore the defendant's serious clinical depression (which might have reduced his powers of self-control) in considering whether an ordinary man would have acted in**

such a way. The House of Lords agreed, Lord Hoffmann said that under s.3 of the 1957 Act, provocation is expressly a matter for the jury and the judge must not tell them to ignore anything they might consider relevant. It is for the jury to decide whether the defendant's behaviour fell below the standard that should have been expected of him: the "ordinary man" is simply a way of illustrating the legal principle that even under provocation; people must conform to an objective standard of behaviour. *Obiter*, the law now recognises that the emotions which may cause loss of self-control (e.g. in battered wives) are not confined to anger but may include fear and despair. Lord Hoffman went on to say that judges should not be required to describe the objective element in provocation by reference to a reasonable man, with or without attribution of personal characteristics, but should explain in simple language the principles of the doctrine of provocation. First, it requires that the accused killed while he had lost self-control and that something caused him to lose self-control. Second, the fact that something caused him to lose self-control is not enough: the law expects people to exercise control over their emotions, and a tendency to violent rages or childish tantrums is a defect in character rather than an excuse. The jury must think that the circumstances were such as to make the loss of self-control sufficiently excusable to reduce the gravity of the offence from murder to manslaughter. In deciding what should count as sufficient, they have to apply what they consider to be appropriate standards of behaviour, making allowance for human nature and the power of the emotions but not allowing someone to rely upon his own violent disposition. In applying these standards of behaviour, the jury represent the community and decide what degree of self-control society is entitled to expect. **Application:** If the jury think that there was some characteristic of the accused, temporary or permanent, which affected the degree of control which society could reasonably have expected of him and which it would be unjust not to take into account, they are at liberty to give effect to this view. If the defendant is mistaken as to the circumstances, he is entitled to be compared with a reasonable man making the same mistake. This appears to be true whether or not the mistake was a reasonable one.

THE CURRENT POSITION

The jury can consider the history of abuse by the victim on the Defendant and the balance of circumstances and characteristics which depends on the defendant's "general capacity for tolerance or self-restraint".

INTOXICATION AND LOSS OF CONTROL

General Principle: There is a difference between a Defendant who is taunted for his drug addiction and a defendant who is simply intoxicated.

R v Morhall [1995] 3 All ER 659
Facts: A habitual glue-sniffer killed another man who nagged him about his habit. The defendant was charged with murder and claimed he had been provoked. **Ratio: Allowing his appeal and substituting a conviction for manslaughter, the House of Lords said there is no rule to prevent a Defendant's relying on a self-induced condition such as drug addiction (or even previous criminal convictions) as characteristics of the ordinary person where these are relevant to the provocation. Application**: Hence, a jury would be asked to consider the effect of such a provocation on a sober alcoholic. However, the Defendant's intoxication would not be taken into account under this defence.

DIMINISHED RESPONSIBILITY

General Principle: Like loss of control, it is only a partial defence which will reduce the conviction from murder to manslaughter.

R v Ahluwalia [1992] 4 All ER 889
Facts: A woman had entered into an "arranged marriage" and had been very badly treated by her husband. He had been violent and

abusive towards her. He had threatened to kill her and had once tried to run her down. He had taunted her about his affair with another woman. One evening the Defendant poured petrol over his bed as he slept and set light to it. She pleaded manslaughter claiming that she had not intended to kill him, just to cause him pain. She was convicted of murder and she appealed. **Ratio: The Court pointed out the presence of a qualifying trigger in the threat to kill expressed by the husband. The issue was whether the defence of provocation as 'sudden and temporary loss of control' might mitigate the sentence of murder. Since the Defendant's action did not immediately follow the husband's provocation, the Court talked about 'slow burn' reaction. Application:** Since the acts of the husband were the qualified trigger, the Court redirected the case to the jury pointing out the question of diminished responsibility due to the Defendant's depression developed after years of abuses.

Salim v Public Prosecutor [2022] SGCA 6 is an intriguing case decided by the Singapore Court of Appeal under the law as it existed before the 2009 Coroners and Justice Act section 52 amendments. In cases where there is evidence that a murder was premeditated, the decision is nevertheless a helpful tool. Could this defence be used in such a scenario, or is it limited to cases where a mental disorder caused a spontaneous decision to kill? The court concluded that if an accused commits a premeditated murder, he may be able to demonstrate that his mental abnormality significantly impaired his mental responsibility for his acts in relation to his crime by demonstrating on the balance of probabilities that it impaired his rationality in deciding to commit the murder. When the decision to commit the crime is said to be aberrant, the defendant must demonstrate that he would not have made that decision if not for his mental disorder. This limitation is necessary to exclude cases in which the accused would have made the same decision even if he had not suffered from the relevant mental disorder. According to the new provision, he must demonstrate that his aberrant reasoning is an explanation for his actions.

THE ABNORMALITY OF MENTAL FUNCTIONING

General Principle: The abnormality of mental functioning must be a contributory factor to the loss of control etc. but need not be the only cause.

R v Byrne [1960] 3 All ER 1
Facts: The Defendant strangled a young woman and mutilated her body. At his trial for murder he brought medical evidence to support his claim that since childhood he had suffered violent and perverted sexual desires that he found it difficult and sometimes impossible to resist. **Ratio: If an abnormality of mental functioning is proved it attracts the defence of diminished responsibility. Application:** The Court of Criminal Appeal quashed the Defendant's conviction for murder and substituted manslaughter; lack of self-control due to an abnormality of mind is capable of constituting diminished responsibility, and the question should have been put to the jury.

ARISING FROM A RECOGNISED MEDICAL CONDITION

General Principle: Alcoholism can cause an abnormality of mind.

R v Tandy [1989] 1 All ER 267
Facts: An alcoholic was charged with the murder of her 11-year-old daughter, but claimed diminished responsibility due to her having drunk a whole bottle of vodka. **Ratio: This defence would be applicable in the case of alcoholics if they have an alcoholic disease or a brain injury that makes drinking completely involuntary. Application:** The Court of Appeal dismissed the Defendant's appeal against a conviction for murder: drunkenness is not an "abnormality of mind", and only if alcoholism had reached such a state that the brain had been injured, or the drinking was purely involuntary, might a defence of diminished responsibility succeed. If the Defendant simply failed to resist an impulse to drink - even if only the first drink was voluntary - she could not avail herself of this defence.

INTOXICATION AND DIMINISHED RESPONSIBILITY

General Principle: When there is no evidence of the defendant suffering from ADS, he might at the time of killing suffer both an abnormality of mental functioning and from the effects of alcohol taken before the killing.

R v Dietschmann [2003] 1 AC 1209
Facts: The Defendant was in a relationship with his much older aunt who was also a drug addict. He was sentenced to prison and his aunt died while he was still there. A month before her death she had given him a watch. He reacted badly to her death and attempted suicide; he was prescribed antidepressants by the doctor. Two weeks after his release he was drinking with two men, they were dancing and the watch fell down and broke. He punched one of the men and kicked him to death. He was convicted of murder and appealed. **Ratio: The House of Lords claimed that it would be impossible for the jury to ignore his intoxicated**

state and decide whether the defendant even sober would have killed as a result of the abnormality. Instead, the jury must first consider the effect of matters other than alcohol and establish whether they amounted to such abnormality of mental functioning that would have prevented the defendant's ability to do one of the things in Section 52(1A). Application:** Hence, the jury should ask themselves whether the defendant satisfied them that, despite the drink, a). he was suffering from a mental abnormality; and b) his mental abnormality substantially impaired his mental responsibility for his fatal acts?

General Principle: The jury can conclude that at the time of the killing the defendant was not suffering from an abnormality, even though ADS is found to exist.

R v Stewart [2009] EWCA Crim 593
Facts: The appellant was a chronic alcoholic sleeping rough in Marble Arch. He killed a man during a fight. He raised the defence of diminished responsibility. **Ratio: The Court of Appeal directed the jury in cases involving ADS. The Court explained that the first step was that the jury must be satisfied that there was an abnormality of mind (which is now abnormality of mental functioning). It is open to the jury to conclude that even though this condition exists, at the time of killing the Defendant was not suffering from any abnormality of mind. And if the jury is satisfied that the defendant was suffering from an abnormality then it must arise from a recognised medical condition. If there is clear evidence, this condition is generally satisfied. Application:** Under the old law, the Court of Appeal directed that the jury must consider another question: whether the ADS considerably damage the defendant's mental responsibility. The Court of Appeal suggested a number of factors: (a) the extent and seriousness of the defendant's dependency (b) the extent to which his ability to control his drinking was reduced (c) whether he was capable of abstinence and if so (d) for how long (e) whether he was choosing for some particular reason (such as a birthday) to decide to get drunk or to drink more than usual.

SUMMARY

- The Defendant must have lost self-control as a result of something (a "qualifying trigger"). The jury must establish that a reasonable person, as the age and sex of the Defendant, might have reacted in the same way.

- The "qualifying trigger" is defined under Section 55 of the Act as the cause of loss of control. There are two different qualifying triggers under this Section: 'a fear of serious violence' and a 'justifiable sense of being seriously wronged'.

- Like loss of control, diminished responsibility is only a partial defence which will reduce the conviction from murder to manslaughter.

Chapter 6 - Non Fatal Offences against the Person

ASSAULT

Assault is a common law offence. A statutory definition of assault does not exist. The best definition of assault comes from the case **Collins v Wilcock** [1984] 3 All ER 374.

General Principle: Assault is an act which causes another person to apprehend the infliction of immediate unlawful force.

Collins v Wilcock [1984] 3 All ER 374
Facts: The Defendant was a prostitute. The Claimant a police officer saw her soliciting men in the street. The police officer stopped her in order to question her, but the Defendant refused and walked away, swearing at him. The police officer took her from the arm and she scratched the Claimant's arm. She was arrested and convicted for assault of a police officer in the execution of his duty. She appealed. **Ratio: According to the definition given by Goff LJ 'an assault is an act which causes another person to apprehend the infliction of immediate, unlawful force. The approaching and shouting are an assault, while the punch is the battery'.** Application: The appeal of the prostitute was allowed. By taking the Defendant from the arm, the police officer committed battery.

General Principle: An assault is committed when the accused 'intentionally, or recklessly, causes another person to apprehend immediate and unlawful personal violence'.

Fagan v Metropolitan Police Commissioner [1968] 3 All ER 442
Facts: A police officer told the Defendant to park his car at a particular place. In doing so the Defendant accidentally drove onto the policeman's foot. The policeman asked the Defendant to remove the car from his foot, but the Defendant switched off the engine and refused to move for some time. The Defendant was

charged with assaulting a constable, and his conviction by magistrates was upheld by Quarter Sessions on the basis of his deliberate failure to move the car. The Divisional Court upheld his conviction but disapproved the reasoning. **Ratio: A mere omission to act cannot amount to an assault. An assault requires a positive act and a failure to act is generally not enough. Nevertheless, whether there is a continuing act that at some point sees the intention of the person to commit an unlawful act, that person is guilty. Application:** From the time the wheel ran onto the policeman's foot until it was removed, and since that was intentional at least in part it was sufficient and the Defendant was convicted.

ACTUS REUS

The *actus reus* of assault consists in an act that causes the victim to apprehend the infliction of immediate, unlawful force.

General Principle: The Defendant must make the victim feel that he can and will carry out threat of force. There is no assault whether it is obvious that the Defendant cannot actually use force.

R v Lamb [1967] 2 All ER 1282
Facts: The Defendant and his friend were playing with a revolver. In the chamber there were two bullets, but neither was opposite the hammer when the Defendant, in jest, pointed the gun at his friend and pulled the trigger. The chamber rotated and the friend was killed. **Ratio: The Court of Appeal said that since the victim shared in the joke, consented to having the gun pointed at him and did not feel threatened (since both believed the gun to be safe at that time) there was no assault and hence no unlawful act on which a charge of manslaughter could be sustained. Application:** The Defendant was not convicted since the element of apprehension of personal violence could not be sustained.

General Principle: If the victim is caused to apprehend such a threat, it is irrelevant that the Defendant does not in fact have the means to carry out that threat.

Logdon v DPP [1976] Crim LR 121

Facts: A Customs officer called on the Defendant to discuss his VAT returns; the Defendant showed the officer a gun in a drawer and told her he would hold her prisoner until money owing him was repaid. The Defendant then handed the gun over and pointed out that it was actually a replica and would not fire, but was charged with assault. **Ratio: It was enough that the victim had reasonable cause to fear that force was about to be inflicted on her; the conditional nature of the implied threat, and the fact that Defendant had neither the means nor the intention of carrying it out, were irrelevant. Application:** The mere apprehension of personal violence was enough to hold the Defendant guilty of assault.

General Principle: The threat of violence must be unlawful and immediate and it can stem from harassing a person by letter and call.

R v Constanza [1997] Crim LR 576, CA

Facts: Evidence against the defendant was that he had stalked his victim for two years, harassing her by repeated telephone calls, letters, unwanted visits and graffiti on her front door, but that he had neither taken nor expressly threatened any immediate physical action against her. **Ratio: The Defendant's actions in sending 800 letters and in doing several calls to the victim amounted to a reasonable cause of apprehension of use of immediate, unlawful force. Application:** He was convicted of assault occasioning actual bodily harm, affirming his conviction, Schiemann LJ said that the defendant lived near the victim's home, and the victim reasonably feared something might happen at any time. It was enough for the prosecution to show a fear of violence at some time not excluding the immediate future.

MENS REA

The *mens rea* required for assault is intention or recklessness to cause another to fear immediate and unlawful personal violence.

General Principle: The Defendant must be intending or being reckless as to cause the victim to apprehend immediate and unlawful personal violence.

R v Venna [1975] 3 All ER 788
Facts: A man was being arrested following a scuffle outside a pub. He kicked out wildly and struck a policeman, breaking a small bone in his hand. The man was convicted of assaulting a constable and his conviction was upheld by the Court of Appeal. **Ratio: The offence of common assault requires intention to cause the victim to apprehend immediate and unlawful personal violence or recklessness as to whether such apprehension is caused. Application:** The acts of the Defendant amounted to *mens rea* of assault.

BATTERY

Battery is the 'actual use of unlawful force on another person without his consent'. Section 39 of the Criminal Justice Act 1988 codifies this common law offence and lays down the procedure and punishments while dealing with the offence.

ACTUS REUS

The *actus reus* of battery consists in the actual infliction of unlawful force on another person.

General Principle: There must be some application of force as this marks the difference between assault and battery.

Collins v Wilcock [1984] 3 All ER 374
Facts: Facts: The Defendant was a prostitute. The Claimant a police officer saw her soliciting men in the street. The police officer stopped her in order to question her, but the Defendant refused and walked away, swearing at him. The police officer took her from the arm and she scratched the Claimant's arm. She was arrested and convicted for assault of a police officer in the

execution of his duty. She appealed. **Ratio: The slightest touch is capable in principle of being an assault, said Goff LJ, though there is a general exception for the exigencies of everyday life. No one can complain about a certain amount of jostling in a supermarket or a busy street, and a party guest must expect to have his hand clasped or his back slapped within reasonable limits. Application:** The Court held that the police officer had committed a battery. The Defendant was not guilty of assault.

General Principle: The application of force need not be aggressive, and the force need not be applied directly.

Haystead v DPP [2000] 3 All ER 890, DC
Facts: A man punched a woman twice in the face, causing the woman to drop the child she had been holding. The child hit his head on the floor. The man was convicted of assaulting the child by beating (i.e. battery). **Ratio: The application of force can also be indirect if the defendant had been reckless. Application:** Affirming the conviction, Laws LJ said that although most batteries are directly inflicted, it is not essential that this should be so. And even if the Defendant did not intend the battery to the child, he was certainly reckless.

MENS REA

The *mens rea* of battery is intention to apply unlawful physical force to another or recklessness as to whether unlawful force is applied.

General Principle: There must be intentional or reckless application of unlawful force upon another.

R v Venna [1975] 3 All ER 788
Facts: A man was being arrested following a scuffle outside a pub. He kicked out wildly and struck a policeman, breaking a small bone in his hand. The man was convicted of assaulting a constable, and his conviction was upheld by the Court of Appeal. **Ratio: The offence of common assault requires intention to cause the victim to apprehend immediate and unlawful**

personal violence or recklessness as to whether such apprehension is caused, or (for battery) intention or recklessness as to the application of force. Application:** The acts of the Defendant amounted to *mens rea* of the offence.

ASSAULT OCCASIONING ACTUAL BODILY HARM

Actual bodily harm refers to the lowest level of injury, disciplined by Section 47 of the Offences against the Person Act 1861. The Section states *'whosoever shall be convicted of any assault occasioning actual bodily harm shall be liable… to imprisonment for five years'*.

ACTUS REUS

The *actus reus* of assault occasioning actual bodily harm requires the establishment of the following elements:

- A valid assault or battery
- That causes
- The actual bodily harm

General Principle: Any hurt or injury calculated to interfere with the health or comfort of the victim amounts to actual bodily harm.

R v Donovan [1934] 2 KB 498
Facts: The Defendant was a man that undertook sexual relationship with a 17-year-old prostitute. He beat her for his own sexual gratification. Two days later a doctor concluded that she had had a fairly severe beating. He was charged with indecent assault and common assault. **Ratio: In the attempt to define the injuries suffered by the prostitute, the court gave a definition of 'bodily harm' as any wound that interferes with the health of a person. The injury does not need to be permanent, but must be more than merely transient and trifling. Application:** The Court of Appeal quashed the conviction on the ground that the trial judge had failed to direct the jury.

General Principle: Physical pain is not a necessary element of actual bodily harm.

DPP v Smith (Michael) [2006] 2 All ER 16
Facts: The Defendant was a guy and the victim his girlfriend. They had an argument and he cut off her ponytail without her consent. Under Section 47 of the OAPA he was charged of actual bodily harm. **Ratio: Whether the Defendant cut off a significant amount of hair may amount to actual bodily harm. Application:** The magistrates held that there was no actual bodily harm. Nevertheless, the case was remitted to the justices since the decision taken by the magistrates was found to be wrong by the Divisional Court.

General Principle: The assault or battery must occasion actual bodily harm.

R v Miller [1954] 2 All ER 529
Facts: The Defendant was charged with assault causing actual bodily harm to his wife. The victim was in a hysterical and nervous condition after being thrown down three times by the Defendant. **Ratio: The judge quoted with approval the words of Archbold that actual bodily harm "includes any hurt or injury calculated to interfere with the health or comfort of the victim", and said that included mental harm as well as physical injury. Application:** It was said that the hurt need not be serious or permanent but must be more than transient and trifling.

MENS REA

Section 47 of the OAPA does not give any definition of the *mens rea* required for actual bodily harm. The *mens rea* uses to assess actual bodily harm is the one of common assault.

General Principle: Whether the Defendant has the intention to apply unlawful force on a person, this amounts to the *mens rea* required to have an offence.

R v Roberts [1971] Crim LR 27

Facts: The Defendant was driving a car. The victim was a passenger at the time he was driving. He made advances to the girl, trying to take her coat off. She got scared, thinking that he was going to commit a more serious assault. She opened the door of the car and jumped from it. She got slightly injured. **Ratio: Even though the Defendant did not intend any injury, he did intend to apply unlawful force on the girl by touching her and by trying to take her coat off. Application:** The court found the Defendant guilty under Section 47.

General Principle: If the Defendant intends to commit assault or battery, or is reckless as to that possibility, and harm results from his actions, it is no defence that he neither intended nor foresaw harm.

R v Savage, R v Parmenter [1991] 4 All ER 698, HL
Facts: The Defendant became involved in an argument in a pub. She threw a pint of beer over the victim's head. The glass slipped from her hand and caused cuts to the victim's wrist. The Court of Appeal allowed her appeal against a conviction for unlawful wounding and substituted assault causing actual bodily harm. **Ratio: The House of Lords said the *mens rea* of assault causing actual bodily harm is no more and no less than the *mens rea* of common assault. It is not necessary to show that the Defendant intended bodily harm or was reckless as to that result. If he intended or was reckless as to the assault, and the actual bodily harm was a reasonably foreseeable result (whether or not it was or should have been foreseen by the Defendant himself), that is sufficient. Application:** A proof of an assault together with proof of the fact that actual bodily harm was occasioned by the assault is enough, the intention to cause actual bodily harm need not be established. The intention to cause assault or battery is enough.

INFLICTING GRIEVOUS BODILY HARM

Section 20 of the Offences Against the Person Act 1861 establishes two offences: malicious wounding and maliciously inflicting grievous bodily harm. *'Whosoever shall unlawfully and maliciously wound or inflict any grievous bodily harm upon any other person, either with or without a weapon or instrument, shall be guilty of an offence and shall be liable ... to imprisonment for not more than five years'*. Comparing to **Section 47**, **Section 20** of the OAPA refers to a more serious offence and requires a higher degree of injury and *mens rea* to be established. The elements required are the following:

- The Defendant must have wounded or
- Inflicted grievous bodily harm; and

- He must have intended some injury or
- Being reckless as to whether some injury would be inflected.

ACTUS REUS

The *actus reus* stems from wounding or causing grievous bodily harm. The Defendant must have inflicted a wound to the victim, such as a cut or a break in the continuity of the whole skin. Wounding does not need the victim to apprehend the infliction of immediate unlawful force.

General Principle: The essence of wounding is that there should be a break in "the whole skin"; a simple fracture that leaves the skin intact is not sufficient, though it may constitute grievous bodily harm.

ICC (a minor) v Eisenhower [1983] 3 All ER 230
Facts: The victim was shot with an airgun pellet just above the eye. The pellet did not penetrate the eye. The victim suffered bruising and internal bleeding into the eye. There was no cut. **Ratio: Whether there is no cut, there is no wound. Wound amounts to break of the whole skin. Application:** The Divisional Court quashed the Defendant's conviction for unlawful wounding, since there was no wound breaking the skin. **Application:** breaking of the skin is important and the actual injury need not be severe.

General Principle: There must be 'wounding' and 'infliction of grievous bodily harm'.

R v Burstow [1997] 4 All ER 225
Facts: A petty officer had a close relationship with a woman after a time she broke it off, but he refused to accept this and began to follow her, telephone her, write menacing letters to her and call at her home. The woman suffered severe clinical depression as a result and the Defendant was charged with inflicting grievous bodily harm. **Ratio: Lord Steyn said that as a matter of current usage, the contextual interpretation of "inflict" can embrace**

the idea of inflicting psychiatric rather than physical injury; the offence can accordingly be committed even where no physical violence is applied directly or indirectly to the body of the victim. Application:** The Court held that like actual bodily harm, grievous bodily harm may be "inflicted" or caused - the two words mean the same - either directly or indirectly. The Defendant's conviction was affirmed.

General Principle: Grievous bodily harm means that the harm is 'really serious'.

R v Brown & Stratton [1998] Crim LR 485, CA
Facts: The Defendants attacked Stratton's father, who had undergone gender reassignment, causing her a broken nose, three broken teeth and a cut over one eye. **Ratio: Grievous bodily harm according to the House of Lords in DPP v Smith means 'really serious harm'. Application:** Affirming the Defendant's conviction, the Court of Appeal said that the jury was entitled to assess the harm as "really serious" so that to be classified as grievous bodily harm.

MENS REA

The *mens rea* required under **Section 20** of the OAPA bases on the intention of the Defendant to cause another person some harm or be subjectively reckless as to whether the victim suffers some harm. In the definition of the offence the term that refers to the *mens rea* required by the Defendant in order to prove his guiltiness is 'maliciously'.

General Principle: 'Maliciously' refers to intention to do the particular kind of harm that was in fact done or recklessness as to whether such harm should occur or not.

R v Cunnigham [1957] 2 All ER 412
Facts: The Defendant tore the gas meter of a house. The intention was to steal the money in it. The gas seeped into the house next door, where a woman got affected by the gas. **Ratio: The concept of recklessness applies to all offences in which the statutory**

definition uses the word 'maliciously'. **Application:** The Defendant was held not guilty of maliciously administering a noxious thing since he did not appreciate the risk of gas escaping to the next-door house.

General Principle: An intention to cause some bodily harm (not necessarily serious) or subjective foresight that some bodily harm may be caused needs to be established.

R v Mowatt [1967] 3 All ER 47
Facts: The Defendant attacked the victim by sitting astride him, raining a series of blows on his face, and lifting his head up and throwing it down again. **Ratio: The offence of grievous bodily harm requires the Defendant to have foreseen the risk of some physical harm. It is enough to establish that the Defendant foresees physical harm to some person may occur. He must foresee some harm. Application:** The Court of Appeal upheld the Defendant's conviction for inflicting grievous bodily harm.

WOUNDING OR CAUSING GRIEVOUS BODILY HARM WITH INTENT

The more serious offence under **Section 18** is causing grievous bodily harm with intent to do grievous bodily harm or to resist arrest and carries a possible life sentence.

General Principle: This offence requires a specific intent to cause grievous bodily harm or to resist arrest. Neither recklessness nor foresight is sufficient.

ACTUS REUS

There must be wounding that causes grievous bodily harm. The meaning of 'wounding' and 'grievous bodily harm' is the same as under **Section 20**.

R v Belfon [1976] 3 All ER 46, CA
Facts: The Defendant pushed a girl to the ground, and he and an accomplice attacked those who came to help her. The Defendant

slashed one man with a razor, causing severe wounds to his head and chest. He was charged with wounding with intent. **Ratio: The Court of Appeal quashed his conviction under s.18 and substituted s.20 unlawful wounding; he had certainly foreseen the risk of such consequences, but it had not been proved that he had the specific intent required for the more serious offence. Application:** This charge was based on wounding rather than grievous bodily harm, but the principle is the same.

MENS REA

This is the differentiating factor between the two offences under **Sections 18** and **20**. Under **Section 20**, it is enough to intend or foresee some harm. Under **section 18** the law intends that the Defendant must actually intend to cause harm which will amount in law to grievous bodily harm. Recklessness is not enough. For example, where the *actus reus* is a wound, intention to wound is not enough. For **section 18** to be satisfied, an intention to cause grievous bodily harm is also important.

POISONING

Section 23 and **Section 24** of the Offences against the Person Act 1861 create offences of unlawfully and maliciously administering or causing to be administered to or taken by any other person any poison or other noxious thing ... so as thereby to endanger the life of that person or inflict grievous bodily harm (**Section 23**), or with the intent to injure, aggrieve or annoy such person (**Section 24**). The maximum penalty for **Section 23** is ten years' imprisonment. The maximum penalty for **Section 24** is five years' imprisonment. The difference between the two Sections is:

- Under Section 23 prosecution must give evidence that the administering of the poison has endangered the life of the victim or inflicted grievous bodily harm.
- Under Section 24 there is no need to show that the poison in fact has had any effect on the victim. Intent to injure is the essential element.

ACTUS REUS

The *actus reus* bases on the administering of a poison directly or indirectly.

General Principle: The proper construction of 'administer' includes conduct which does not use the application of direct force to the victim nevertheless brings the noxious thing into contact with his body.

R v Gillard [1988] 87 Cr App R 189
Facts: The Defendants were three men charged with conspiracy to administer a noxious substance by spraying CS gas into the face of their chosen victim, a doorman at a wine bar. **Ratio: The Court of Appeal considered the meaning of the word 'administer'. Lord McNeill held that, "The word 'takes' postulates some 'ingestion' by the victim; 'administer' must have some other meaning and there is no difficulty in including in that meaning such conduct as spraying the victim with noxious fluid or vapour, whether from a device such as a gas canister, or for example, hosing down with effluent. There is no necessity when the word 'administer' is used to postulate any form of entry into the victim's body, whether through any orifice or by absorption." Application:** Since the element of valid *actus reus* was established, the court affirmed the convictions of the three men.

General Principle: A substance is noxious if it is 'hurtful, unwholesome or objectionable'.

R v Pollard [1992] HCA 69
Facts: A 23-year-old woman for a joke put a small amount of cannabis (enough for ten cigarettes) into a chocolate cake cooked by her aunt. Some family members who ate the cake hallucinated or became ill. **Ratio: Whether the thing administered is noxious or poisonous or destructive will depend on each case and the jury should take into account all the circumstances including the nature of the substance and the quantity given. Application:** The woman was charged with and convicted of administering a noxious substance with intent to injure, aggrieve or annoy under Section 24.

MENS REA

General Principle: Prosecution must prove that the Defendant intended to injure, aggrieve or annoy either by the effects of the administration itself or by some ulterior motive.

R v Hill [1986] 83 Cr App R 386
Facts: The Defendant gave a drug to two boys, intending to render them susceptible to his homosexual advances. **Ratio: It is necessary to have regard not merely to his intent with regard to the effect which the noxious thing will have upon the person to whom it is administered, but to his whole object in acting as he has done. Application:** The Court of Appeal quashed his conviction under Section 24, but the House of Lords restored it. The trial judge's direction had quite clearly distinguished between an intention to injure (in relation to the whole of Defendant's plan) and a benevolent intention such as keeping a child awake to enjoy late night fireworks: there was overwhelming evidence that the Defendant's intention was the former, and the jury had quite properly convicted.

SUMMARY

- The non-fatal offences against the person are assault, battery, assault causing actual bodily harm, infliction of grievous bodily harm, wounding or causing grievous bodily harm with intent and poisoning.
- Assault is a common law offence. It is an act that causes another person to apprehend the infliction of immediate unlawful force.
- Battery is the actual use of unlawful force against a person without consent.
- **Section 47** states that assault that causes a person to get injured by interfering with the victim's health and comfort amounts to assault causing actual bodily harm.
- **Section 20** describe infliction of grievous bodily harm as unlawfully and maliciously wound or inflict any grievous bodily harm upon any other person.
- The more serious offence under **Section 18** is causing grievous bodily harm with intent to do grievous bodily harm or to resist arrest and carries a possible life sentence.

- The OAPA 1861 creates two offences under Sections 23 and 24 that refer to poisoning.

Chapter 7 - Sexual Offences

INTRODUCTION

The law on sexual offences has recently undergone drastic changes after the introduction of the Sexual Offences Act 2003. The Act came into force on the 1st of May 2004. The statutory provision has completely changed the law relating to sexual offences and in most part repeals the old law and places most of the common law on statutory balance. It recreated many offences and redefined and extended the existing ones.

RAPE

This offence has been codified under **Section 1** of the Act.

Its definition stems from **Section 1(1)** that states:

(1) A person commits an offence if -
(a) he intentionally penetrates the vagina, anus or mouth of another person (B) with his penis,
(b) B does not consent to the penetration, and (c) A does not reasonably believe that B consents.
(2) Whether a belief is reasonable is to be determined having regard to all the circumstances,
including any steps A has taken to ascertain whether B consents.
(3) Sections 75 and 76 apply to an offence under this section.
(4) A person guilty of an offence under this section is liable, on conviction on indictment, to
imprisonment for life.

- *ACTUS REUS*

By looking at the Definition given in **Section 1(1)** of the Sexual Offences Act 2003, the *actus reus* element amounts to penetration of the vagina, anus or mouth of another person with the penis without consent.

- **THERE HAS TO BE PENILE PENETRATION**

The question whether penetration has occurred will be decided by the jury. Even a slight degree of penetration is sufficient. According to **Section 79(2)** of the Sexual Offences Act 2003 'penetration is a continuing act from entry to withdrawal'.

General Principle: Oral penetration is not less serious than vaginal or anal rape.

R v Ismail [2005] EWCA Crim 397
Facts: The Defendant was a 18-year-old boy that sexually assaulted a 16-year-old virgin. He touched her vagina and then forced her to suck his penis and ejaculated in her mouth, threatening to stab her. The victim managed to call the emergency services on her mobile phone. The assault was recorded. He was charged for sexual assault under Section 1 of the Sexual Offences Act 2003. **Ratio: The court pointed out that the fact that this was oral rape did not make it any less serious than vaginal or anal rape. Application:** The Defendant was convicted and sentenced to six years' detention.

General principle: Whether the victim initially consents to the sexual relationship and then subsequently withdraws and the intercourse continues, the Defendant will be liable.

R v Cooper and Schaub [1994] Crim LR 531
Facts: The two Defendants met the victim in a nightclub. At the end of the evening, that offered to take her home. She fell asleep in the back of the car. When she woke up she found one of the two Defendant trying to have sexual intercourse with her. The second Defendant put his penis in her mouth. Prosecution alleged that she did not consent to any of the sexual activity. The defense was that she consented. **Ratio: By directing the jury, the judge stated that whether initially there was consent to intercourse and this was subsequently withdrawn and intercourse continued, rape was still committed. Application:** The Defendants were convicted.

- **TRANSSEXUALS**

The Sexual Offences Act 2003 has made the law gender neutral. **Section 79(3)** states that 'References to a part of the body include references to apart surgically constructed (in particular, through gender reassignmentsurgery)'. Hence, females who have undergone penile surgery may be convicted of rape.

- **ORAL PENETRATION**

The old law did not include oral penetration as an element of rape. The definition of rape under the Sexual Offences Act has been extended to include oral penetration.

- **CONSENT**

Consent arises as a part of *mens rea* (the Defendant did not reasonably believe that the complainant was consenting) and as a part of *actus reus* (it has to be proved that the complainant did not consent). Under the Sexual Offences Act 2003, there are three ways by which consent is presumed to be absent: under the definition of consent provided in section 74, or under the statutory presumptions under section 75 and 76.

- **CONSENT UNDER SECTION 74**

Section 74 – a person consents if he agrees by choice and has the freedom and capacity to make that choice.

General Principle: The Defendant 'agrees by choice' to have sexual intercourse with the defendant and there must be a positive agreement as opposed to the mere lack of protest.

R v Olugboja [1981] 3 All ER 443
Facts: A man raped a woman and then took her companion into another room to rape her. The man's companion now told the same

woman that he too was going to have sex with her, and told her to take off her trousers. The woman did so because she was frightened, and allowed this man to have sex with her without resisting. The man was convicted of rape, and his conviction was upheld by the Court of Appeal. **Ratio: Consent is not the same as reluctant submission, and since no clear line can be drawn it is a matter for the jury; they must decide whether the victim consented (in the everyday sense of that word) or not. The woman must not only make the choice to have sexual intercourse, she must also have the freedom to choose. Therefore, where the woman has consented under a threat of violence is no consent. Application:** The Court of Appeal dismissed the appeal, affirming conviction of the Defendant. Submission induced by force, fear or fraud was not consent.

General Principle: Consent is free choice.

R v Jheeta [2007] EWCA Crim 1699
Facts: The victim and the Defendant had been in a sexual relationship. The girl decided it to end it. The Defendant started sending her anonymous threatening messages. The girl got scared and sought protection from the Defendant. This allowed him to prolong the sexual relationship. When the mental scheme was found out, the victim sued the Defendant for several rapes. **Ratio: The victim's apparent consent was not a free choice. Application:** The court convicted the Defendant. His conviction was affirmed by the Court of Appeal.

General Principle: the non-use of condom or its removal without the victim's consent amounts to rape.

Assange v Sweden [2011] EWHC 2849
Facts: Julian Assange, the Australian journalist, gave a lecture in Sweden. He had sex with two women. Both of them complained at the police. The allegation was that he had unprotected intercourse with a woman that consented to it but only with the use of a condom. **Ratio: Whether a woman consents to an intercourse only with the use of a condom, failure to do so amounts to rape. Application:** The Swedish issued a European

Arrest Warrant. By the time, Assange was living in the UK where a district judge ordered his extradition to Sweden. Assange found political asylum in Ecuador.

* **CAPACITY TO MAKE A CHOICE**

The parties must have the capacity to make the choice.

General Principle: Whether the victim, although very drunk, had retained the capacity to consent, intoxication does not allow the victim to claim to have been raped.

R v Bree [2007] 2 All ER 676
Facts: The Defendant visited his brother at his student flat. The Defendant went out with the girl flat mate and the brother's girlfriend. The four of them consumed a large amount of alcohol. When they came back to the flat, the Defendant and the girl flatmate initiated a sexual intercourse. According to the Defendant she consented. On the contrary the girl stated that she was too drunk to give consent. **Ratio: It was held by the Court of Appeal that, "If, through drink (or for any other reason) the complainant has temporarily lost her capacity to choose whether to have intercourse on the relevant occasion, she is not consenting, and subject to questions about the Defendant's state of mind, if intercourse takes place, this would be rape. However, where the complainant has voluntarily consumed even substantial quantities of alcohol, but nevertheless remains capable of choosing whether or not to have intercourse, and in drink agrees to do so, this would not be rape. We should perhaps underline that, as a matter of practical reality, capacity to consent may evaporate well before a complainant becomes unconscious. Whether this is soon or not, however, is fact specific, or more accurately, depends on the actual state of mind of the individuals involved on the particular occasion." Application:** This question largely depends on the facts of the particular case. At trial the Defendant

was convicted for rape but the sentence was then quashed by the Court of Appeal.

- **EVIDENTIAL PRESUMPTIONS UNDER SECTION 75**

The evidential burden is on the Defendant to adduce evidence to prove that the presumption does not apply in his case and these evidential presumptions can be rebutted. The evidential presumptions are:

(i)   that the complainant did not consent to the penetration, and

(ii)   that the Defendant did not reasonably believe that the complainant consented.

Section 75 - *Evidential presumptions about consent*

(1) If in proceedings for an offence to which this section applies it is proved—
(a) that the defendant did the relevant act,
(b) that any of the circumstances specified in subsection (2) existed, and
(c) that the defendant knew that those circumstances existed, the complainant is to be taken not to have consented to the relevant act unless sufficient evidence is adduced to raise an issue as to whether he consented, and the defendant is to be taken not to have reasonably believed that the complainant consented unless sufficient evidence is adduced to raise an issue as to whether he reasonably believed it.
(2) The circumstances are that—
(a) any person was, at the time of the relevant act or immediately before it began, using violence against the complainant or causing the complainant to fear that immediate violence would be used against him;
(b) any person was, at the time of the relevant act or immediately before it began, causing the
complainant to fear that violence was being used, or that immediate violence would be used,

against another person;

(c) the complainant was, and the defendant was not, unlawfully detained at the time of the relevant act;

(d) the complainant was asleep or otherwise unconscious at the time of the relevant act;

(e) because of the complainant's physical disability, the complainant would not have been able at the time of the relevant act to communicate to the defendant whether the complainant consented;

(f) any person had administered to or caused to be taken by the complainant, without the complainant's consent, a substance which, having regard to when it was administered or taken, was capable of causing or enabling the complainant to be stupefied or overpowered at the time of the relevant act.

(3) In subsection (2)(a) and (b), the reference to the time immediately before the relevant act began is, in the case of an act which is one of a continuous series of sexual activities, a reference to the time immediately before the first sexual activity began.

- ## CONCLUSIVE PRESUMPTIONS UNDER S76

These presumptions only arise when the prosecution has proved beyond reasonable doubt that the Defendant did the 'relevant act'. The presumption is conclusive and may not be rebutted by evidence to the contrary.

General Principle: The complainant has not consented where the Defendant intentionally deceives the complainant as to the nature or purpose of the act of penetration.

R v Williams [1922] All ER 433
Facts: The Defendant was a singing teacher whose 16-year-old pupil allowed him to have sex with her after he told her it was just a way of improving the quality of her voice. **Ratio: In case of deception, the consent is vitiated. Application:** The Defendant's conviction for rape was upheld on appeal. The complainant had not consented to sexual intercourse because she did not know that was what the defendant intended. Her consent was obtained by

fraud as to the nature of the act and hence her consent was not valid.

General Principle: The Defendant intentionally induces the complainant to consent to the penetration by impersonating someone known personally to the complainant.

R v Elbekkay [1995] Crim LR 163
Facts: It was agreed that the Defendant should stay overnight at the house where his friend lived with his girlfriend. After his friend had fallen asleep, the Defendant went into the girl's bedroom and began to have sex with her; she made no protest initially, thinking it was her boyfriend, but when she realized the truth she protested vigorously. **Ratio: It had long been established that a man commits rape if he obtains her consent to sex by impersonating her husband, and in modern society the same principle should clearly be extended to the impersonation of any permanent sexual partner. Application:** The Defendant was convicted of rape, and his appeal was dismissed.

- *MENS REA*

General Principle: The *mens rea* of rape is that the Defendant knows the victim is not consenting, or is reckless as to the possibility that she may not be. It is not entirely clear whether this recklessness is subjective or objective.

There are two ways in which the prosecution can prove that the Defendant did not reasonably believe that the complainant was consenting: by proving that either the evidential or conclusive presumptions under **Section 75** and **Section 76** are applicable or by relying on **Section 1(1)(c)**.

- **THE POSITION BEFORE THE SEXUAL OFFENCES ACT 2003**

DPP v Morgan [1975] 2 All ER 347

Facts: The Defendant invited three friends back to his house one evening to have sex with his wife. He told them she would put up a show of resistance, but that this was for her own gratification and she actually consented. The three had sex with the wife, who did resist, and were subsequently charged with rape. **Ratio: Upholding their convictions, the House of Lords said an honest but mistaken belief in the Defendant's consent would be enough to negate rape, but in the instant case the jury clearly had not believed the men's story. This subjective approach was criticized by some. The Sexual Offences Act 2003 has attempted to find a compromise between a subjective and an objective approach. Application:** Upholding their convictions, the House of Lords said an honest but mistaken belief in the Defendant's consent would be enough to negate rape.

ASSAULT BY PENETRATION

There are five elements which have to be proved to establish this offence. This offence was introduced by **Section 2** of the Sexual Offences Act 2003. It carries a maximum life sentence. Penetration must be with the part of the body or anything else. This is helpful in cases when the complainant is not sure whether the penetration was penile or another part of his body or an instrument was used. The defendant will still be liable for a serious offence which carries the same maximum sentence as rape. This however only applies to penetration of the vagina or the anus, oral penetration is not sufficient.

General Principle: Assault by penetration is an offence no matter what part of the body is used as long as it is proved that the victim did not consent.

R v Coomber [2005] EWCA Crim 1113
Facts: The Defendant was a single man that had been a scout leader for a number of years and member of a local club. At the club he met a lady with his son. They became friends and on two occasions the son was allowed to stay over the Defendant's home. On the Defendant's computer the police found images of him abusing the boy. **Ratio: Even penetration with a finger falls into**

the definition of Section 2 of the Sexual Offences Act 2003.
Application: The Defendant was convicted for rape.

General Principle: Penetration must be 'sexual'.

The test is codified in **Section 8** of the Act. The test was based on the following decision:

R v Court [1988] 2 All ER 221
Facts: A man pulled a 12-year-old girl over his knee and hit her bottom twelve times over her shorts. He admitted he had a 'buttock fetish'. He was charged with indecent assault (now sexual assault. **Ratio: Under Section 78(a) the jury will consider whether a reasonable person would regard the nature of the penetration as sexual, irrespective of the circumstances or the defendant's purpose. The House of Lords held that an objective test be applied to the word 'indecent'. Application:** Spanking a person was held to fall into the definition of 'indecent assault'.

- **ABSENCE OF CONSENT**

The prosecution must prove that the complainant did not consent to the penetration. The same meaning of consent under rape is applies here, even Section 75 and Section 76 are available under this section.

MENS REA

- **INTENTIONAL PENETRATION**

The prosecution must prove that the penetration was intentional (but it does not need to be proved that the defendant intended it to be sexual).

- **ABSENCE OF REASONABLE BELIEF IN CONSENT**

As with rape, the prosecution has to prove that the Defendant did not believe that the complainant was consenting to penetration.

- **SEXUAL ASSAULT**

This is also a new offence under Section 3 of the Sexual Offences Act 2003. It carries a maximum sentence of ten years imprisonment. There are five elements which need to be proved by the prosecution to establish the *actus reus* of the offence.

ACTUS REUS

- **TOUCHING**

General Principle: The prosecution must prove that the Defendant touched the complainant.

R v H [2005] EWCA Crim 732
Facts: The Defendant approached the complainant and asked her if she wanted to have sexual intercourse with him. She refused and walked away; he approached her again and asked her if she was

shy. He then took hold of her tracksuit and tried to pull her towards himself. **Ratio: It was held by Lord Woolf that, "It is important to note that the opening words of section 79(8) are 'touching includes touching' and in particular 'through anything'. Subsection (8) is not a definition section. We have no doubt that it was not Parliament's intention by the use of that language to make it impossible to regard as a sexual assault touching which took place by touching what the victim was wearing at the time."**

Application: Hence, touching could include 'touching' what the victim was wearing at that time.

General Principle: Touching must be 'sexual'.

As with assault by penetration, the prosecution must prove that the touching was sexual. Section 78 also applies to the meaning of the word 'sexual'.

General Principle: There must be an absence of Consent.

The prosecution must prove that the complainant did not consent to the touching. Section 75 and 76 are also applicable to sexual assault. 075238741

MENS REA

General Principle: There must be intentional touching and absence of reasonable belief in consent

The prosecution must prove that the touching was intentional (but it does not need to be proved that the defendant intended it to be sexual). As with rape and assault by penetration, the prosecution has to prove that the defendant did not believe that the complainant was consenting to touching.

CAUSING SEXUAL ACTIVITY WITHOUT CONSENT

This is a new offence introduced by Section 4 of the Sexual Offences Act 2003. It carries a maximum penalty of ten years' imprisonment unless Section 3(4) is applicable then the maximum sentence is life imprisonment. There are five elements that need to be proved by the prosecution in order to establish this offence.

ACTUS REUS

- **CAUSING A PERSON TO ENGAGE IN SEXUAL ACTIVITY**

This offence was introduced to deal with situations where the Defendant forces the complainant to engage in a sexual act against their wishes. For example,forcing the complainant to have sexual intercourse with the defendant oranother person, or forcing the complainant to masturbate himself or thedefendant.

General Principle: The complainant must have been 'caused' to engage in 'sexual activity' and there must be absence of consent

As with assault by penetration and sexual assault, the prosecution must prove that the sexual activity was sexual. Section 78 also applies to the meaning of the word 'sexual'.The prosecution must prove that the complainant did not consent to engaging in the sexual activity.Section 75 and 76 are also applicable to the offence of causing a person to engage in sexual activity.

MENS REA

- **INTENTIONALLY CAUSING THE PERSON TO ENGAGE IN A SEXUAL ACTIVITY**

The prosecution must prove that defendant intentionally caused the complainant to engage in the sexual activity (but it does not need to be proved that the defendant intended it to be sexual).

- **ABSENCE OF REASONABLE BELIEF IN CONSENT**

As with rape and assault by penetration and sexual assault, the prosecution has to prove that the defendant did not believe that the complainant was consenting to engaging in the sexual activity.

SUMMARY

- The law on sexual offences has recently undergone drastic changes after the introduction of the Sexual Offences Act 2003.

- One sexual offence is rape whose definition stems from **Section 1(1)** of the Act.

- Transsexual unlawful relationships fall within the category of sexual offences.

- The new law includes oral penetration as an element of rape.

- The element of consent establishes whether there is involuntary sexual intercourse. The parties must have the capacity to make the choice.

- The prosecution must prove that the penetration was intentional.

- Causing sexual activity without consent is a new offence, introduced to deal with situations where the Defendant forces the complainant to engage in a sexual act against their wishes.

Chapter 8 - Manslaughter

Introduction

Involuntary manslaughter includes all kinds of unlawful homicide other than murder. Any form of unlawful killing where there is no proof of malice.

Three are the possible types of manslaughter:

1. Constructive

2. Gross negligence

3. Reckless

General Principle: The major point of difference between murder and involuntary manslaughter is that involuntary manslaughter does not include 'malice afterthought'.

Andrews v DPP [1937] AC 576

Facts: A van driver killed a pedestrian by careless driving and was charged with manslaughter.

Ratio: Lord Atkin while trying to explain the difference between murder and manslaughter explained, "Of all crimes manslaughter appears to afford most difficulties of definition, for it concerns homicide in so many and so varying conditions... the law...recognises murder on one hand based mainly, though not exclusively, on an intention to kill, and manslaughter on the other hand, based mainly, though not exclusively, on the absence of intent to kill, but with the presence of an element of "unlawfulness" which is the elusive factor". Application: There is an obvious difference in the law of manslaughter between doing an unlawful act and doing a lawful act with a degree of carelessness that the legislature makes criminal.

CONSTRUCTIVE/ (UNLAWFUL ACT) MANSLAUGHTER

Whether the Defendant kills by an unlawful and dangerous act someone, he will be convicted of constructive manslaughter. The elements required in order to establish constructive manslaughter are the following:

- Commitment of an unlawful act
- Dangerous
- Intended to be committed
- That causes the death of someone.

AN INTENTIONAL ACT

It must be proved that the Defendant intended to commit the unlawful act but foreseeability that the act may cause the death or harm of someone is not required.

General Principle: The Defendant lacks the *mens rea* for murder but kills someone while committing an unlawful (criminal) act.

DPP v Newbury and Jones [1977] AC 500
Facts: As a train approached a bridge two teenage boys pushed a piece of a paving slab over the parapet of the bridge. The stone struck the train and went through the window, killing the guard, and the boys were charged with manslaughter. **Ratio: The Defendant can be convicted of manslaughter by an unlawful act even if he did not foresee his act might cause harm to another. He need not be aware that his act was unlawful, as long as he realises what he is doing, and he need not intend (or even consider the risk of) death or injury. Application:** Upholding their conviction, the House of Lords pointed out that there must be an intentional (voluntary) unlawful act in order to prove the offence.

General Principle: The intentional act must result in the death of a person but there need not have been any intention to cause harm.

R v Le Brun [1991] 4 All ER 673
Facts: A man hit his wife on the chin (without meaning any serious harm) in an argument outside their house. When she fell unconscious, he dragged her away to avoid detection and in so

doing caused her head to hit the pavement sufficiently hard to fracture her skull, as a result of which she died. **Ratio: Although the intentional unlawful act was not the direct cause of death. That act and the act causing death were part of "the same sequence of events", and that was sufficient. Application:** The man's intention not to kill his wife was irrelevant; his intentional act of hitting caused the death of his wife.

AN UNLAWFUL ACT

A tort is not enough, and neither is an inherently lawful act (such as driving) that becomes unlawful only because it is badly done and/or causes death.

General Principle: The act must be genuinely unlawful in the criminal sense.

R v Scarlett [1993] 4 All ER 629
Facts: A publican used some force to eject a drunk man from his premises; perhaps because of his drunkenness, the man fell backwards down a flight of steps, struck his head, and died from his injuries. **Ratio: Allowing the defendant's appeal, the Court of Appeal said that the objective test of a dangerous act is independent of the possibly subjective test of unlawfulness; if in these circumstances the defendant used no more force that was necessary in the circumstances as he honestly believed them to be, he was not guilty of manslaughter and accordingly the defendant's conviction for unlawful act manslaughter was quashed. Application:** The unlawful act will be an offence against the person but it can also be an offence such as criminal damage as long as there is a causal link and it is dangerous.

General Principle: The act must be objectively dangerous, such as all sober and reasonable people would inevitably recognise that it will subject another person to at least the risk of some harm resulting therefrom, albeit not necessarily serious harm.

R v Dawson [1985] 81 Cr App R 150, CA

Facts: The Defendants carried out an armed robbery at a petrol station late one night. The 60-year-old attendant pressed an alarm button and the robbers ran away, but shortly after the police arrived the attendant collapsed and died from a heart attack. **Ratio: The Defendants were charged with manslaughter, but their conviction was quashed by the Court of Appeal. They had not intended any physical harm, and causing emotional disturbance was not "an act likely to cause harm" for the purpose of manslaughter, since a reasonable man would not have thought that any physical harm was a likely result. Watkins LJ said the test can only be undertaken upon the basis of the knowledge gained by the sober and reasonable man as though he were present at the scene. Application:** The Defendant could become liable if he became aware of special knowledge during the commission of the offence which could make the act dangerous.

General Principle: A reasonable man test will applicable whether in the same circumstances as the defendant a reasonable man must have foreseen that some harm would come to another person.

R v Watson [1989] 2 All ER 865
Facts: The Defendants broke into a house where an 87-year-old man lived alone, intending to steal. They confronted him as he awoke, abused him verbally, and then left. The man died of heart failure 90 minutes later, and the defendants were charged with manslaughter on the basis of their unlawful act of burglary. **Ratio: The trial judge told the jury that in deciding whether the act was dangerous they should take the point of view of a reasonable bystander with the knowledge available to the defendant; there was no evidence that the defendant knew the victim's age or state of health when they first broke in, but it must have become obvious to them once they saw him. The Court of Appeal quashed the conviction on a question of causation, but approved the judge's direction as regards the dangerous act. Application:** The Defendants' act was dangerous even in the view of a reasonable bystander and hence fulfilled the *actus reus.*

General Principle: There must be an act rather than an omission.

R v Lowe [1973] QB 702

Facts: A man of low intelligence neglected a baby belonging to his partner, which died of dehydration after ten days. He was charged with wilful neglect contrary to s.1 of the *Children & Young Persons Act 1933*, and with manslaughter, and convicted on both counts. **Ratio: Affirming the former conviction and quashing the latter, Phillimore LJ said mere neglect, even though a statutory crime was not sufficient for unlawful act manslaughter if the defendant had not foreseen the consequences of his neglect. Application:** The Defendant's omission to do something does not attract the charge of manslaughter.

General Principle: The act does not have to be specifically aimed at the victim

R v Goodfellow [1986] 83 Cr App R 23

Facts: A man set fire to his council house, hoping to be moved to a better one, but his wife, one of his children, and another woman died in the fire. **Ratio: The man was convicted of manslaughter, and the Court of Appeal dismissed his appeal on the grounds that arson is clearly an unlawful dangerous act on which a conviction can properly be based. Application:** All that is needed, once causation is established, is an act creating a risk to anyone.

General Principle: The unlawful act must have caused the death of the victim.

R v Cato [1976] 1 All ER 260, CA

Facts: Two heroin users injected one another several times during the course of one night, and the one of them died in the morning. **Ratio: The Defendant was convicted of manslaughter, and the Court of Appeal upheld his conviction even though his acts were not "directed against" anyone, his friend having freely**

consented. **The unlawful and dangerous act, said Lord Widgery CJ, was administering a noxious substance which caused the victim's death. Application:** Consent by the victim was no defence to this.

General Principle: The unlawful act must have both factually and legally caused the death of the victim.

R v Corbett [1996] Crim LR 594
Facts: A man was convicted of manslaughter: following an argument he had head-butted the victim, causing the victim to fall into the gutter where he was struck and killed by a passing car. **Ratio: The Court of Appeal affirmed the conviction and said this was a foreseeable result of the defendant's assault. The assault could thus be regarded as a cause of the death. Application:** The unlawful act must have caused the death of the victim.

MANSLAUGHTER BY GROSS NEGLIGENCE

This occurs when death is caused as a result of the Defendant's gross negligence, in circumstances where he has a duty to take care and fails to do so. The elements of the offence are the following:

- presence of a duty of care
- breach of the duty due to gross negligence
- that causes the death of a person

DUTY OF CARE

As per the case **Donoughue v Stevenson** [1932] AC 562 a duty of care is owed to the so-called neighbour, a person that is so closely and directly affected by a negligent act that it ought reasonably to have been taken in consideration.

General Principle: There is a comprehensive duty not to cause physical harm to other people by one's actions, and in some

specific circumstances there may be a duty not to allow physical harm to occur by inaction.

R v Singh [1999] Crim LR 582

Facts: The manager of a privately-owned block of flats was convicted of manslaughter after one of the tenants died of carbon monoxide poisoning. There was evidence that the gas fires in many of the flats were unsafe, and there had been complaints from other tenants (though not from the victim). **Ratio: The Court of Appeal agreed that the Defendant had a duty of care and affirmed a suspended prison sentence. Application:** The Defendant had a duty of care towards the tenants and he was liable for neglecting his duty.

General Principle: The tortious principle of '*ex turpi causa non oritur actio*' is not available in criminal cases.

R v Wacker [2003] 4 All ER 295

Facts: A lorry driver caused the deaths of 58 illegal immigrants travelling in the back of his lorry by thoughtlessly blocking their only ventilation inlet. He was convicted of manslaughter and sentenced to six years' imprisonment on each count, to run consecutively with an eight-year sentence for conspiring to smuggling immigrants. **Ratio: The principle that the Claimant will not be allowed any legal remedy if it arises in connection with his own illegal act is not available in criminal cases. Application:** The Defendant claimed that law of negligence was not applicable to parties of a criminal enterprise. The Court of Appeal declined this reasoning and stated the tortuous principle of '*ex turpi causa non oritur actio*' was not applicable in criminal cases.

General Principle: The Negligence must have caused the death of the victim and had the Defendant exercised proper care the death would not have occurred.

R v Armstrong [1989] Crim LR 149

Facts: A drug addict supplied another man with heroin and equipment. This man (who had already drunk a large amount of alcohol) injected himself with heroin and died shortly afterwards. At the Defendant's trial for manslaughter, there was conflicting evidence as to whether the heroin contributed to the victim's death or whether the victim would have died from the alcohol alone. **Ratio: The negligence of the Defendant must be the cause of the death the victim and if the cause of death is not established the Defendant will be acquitted. Application: The** judge directed an acquittal: if the experts were not sure as to the cause of death, he said, the jury could not possibly be.

General Principle: There must be gross negligence.

R v Church [1965] 2 All ER 72
Facts: After unsuccessful sex with a woman in a van, the Defendant attacked her and knocked her unconscious. The Defendant tried to revive her without success, and after about half an hour, thinking she was dead, he panicked and threw her body into a nearby river. She was not in fact dead but died from drowning, and the defendant was charged with manslaughter. **Ratio: Sometimes, the court will categorise the acts of the Defendant as forming a transaction, it is enough for the Defendant to have *mens rea* at any one point during the transaction. The Defendant in this case was found guilty under the transaction principle. Application:** Edmund Davies J said he was guilty of criminal negligence in not checking whether the woman was still alive, and that in any case the woman died of an unlawful dangerous act.

General principle: The question which the jury has to decide whether the conduct of the Defendant was so bad that it amounts to a criminal act or omission.

R v Adomako [1994] 3 All ER 79
Facts: The Defendant was an anaesthetist. During an operation, the breathing tube accidentally became detached from the machine and the supply of oxygen to the patient was stopped. The Defendant did not notice this for almost five minutes, until the patient's heart also stopped and an alarm sounded. The patient could not be resuscitated, and the defendant was charged with

manslaughter. **Ratio: The ordinary principles of the law of negligence, said Lord Mackay LC, apply to ascertain whether or not the Defendant has been in breach of a duty of care towards the victim who has died. If such breach of duty is established the next question is whether that breach of duty caused the death of the victim. If so, the jury must go on to consider whether that breach of duty should be characterised as gross negligence and therefore as a crime. This will depend on the seriousness of the breach of duty committed by the Defendant in all the circumstances in which the Defendant was placed when it occurred. The essence of the matter, which is supremely a jury question, is whether, having regard to the risk of death involved, the conduct of the Defendant was as bad in all the circumstances as to amount in their judgment to a criminal act or omission. Application:** It is for the jury to decide whether the conduct of the Defendant was so bad so as to amount to a criminal act or omission.

General Principle: In cases of corporate manslaughter, there must be evidence to show that an identifiable human being has been negligent.

Attorney-General's Reference (No.2 of 1999) [2000] 3 All ER 182

Facts: Great Western Trains were charged with manslaughter following a rail crash in which seven people were killed, but the judge directed their acquittal on finding no evidence that the managing director or any other named senior officer of the company had been sufficiently negligent. **Ratio: On a reference by the Attorney-General, the Court of Appeal said that as the law now stands there is no separate offence of "corporate manslaughter". A non-human Defendant such as a company cannot be convicted of manslaughter unless there is evidence to show the guilt of an identifiable human being for the same crime. Application:** The Court of Appeal held that proof of gross negligence did not require proof of any particular state of mind and did not require evidence as to the accused's state of mind but it did require an identifiable human being.

SUMMARY

- Involuntary manslaughter includes all kinds of unlawful homicide other than murder. Any form of unlawful killing where there is no proof of malice.

- It must be proved that the Defendant intended to commit the unlawful act but foreseeability that the act may cause the death or harm of someone is not required.

- Whether the Defendant's gross negligence, in circumstances where he has a duty to take care and fails to do so, causes the harm of someone, he will be guilty of manslaughter by gross negligence.

Chapter 9 - Defences

INTRODUCTION

Criminal law makes no distinction between intoxication by drink or by drugs and it is no defence in itself, but has frequently to be considered either as leading to a lack of *mens rea* or as the cause of a mistake that may offer a defence. The law is unsympathetic towards those who injure others or their property while under the influence of drink or drugs taken voluntarily.

INVOLUNTARY INTOXICATION

The principle of intoxication allows the Defendant to use evidence of his intoxication to prove that he did not form the necessary *mens rea* for the offence. In those circumstances where the Defendant has been involuntarily intoxicated so that he lacks the *mens rea* required to validate the offence, he will be acquitted.

General Principle: When intoxication is involuntary, then this defence is available for any offence (both specific and basic intent crimes).

R v Kingston [1994] 3 All ER 353, HL
Facts: A man with homosexual paedophilic tendencies went to the flat of another man. Unknown to the man, the owner of the flat intended to lure him into a compromising situation in order to blackmail him, and drugged his coffee. He then took him into a bedroom where there was a 15-year-old boy, also drugged. The man performed various acts with the boy and was subsequently charged with indecent assault. **Ratio: If *mens rea* has been established in an intoxicated state, it is no defence to claim that the offence would not have been committed in a sober state.** **Application:** Potts J directed the jury that the man's intoxication was irrelevant, and that a drugged intent was still intent, and the jury convicted. The Court of Appeal allowed the man's appeal but the House of Lords restored the conviction. It is no answer, said Lord Mustill, for the Defendant to say that he would not have done what he did had he been sober, provided always that whatever

element of intent is required by the offence is proved to have been present.

VOLUNTARY INTOXICATION

It is very rare that voluntary intoxication will be use as a valid defence. Nevertheless, in those circumstances where the Defendant's intoxication is proven to be so extreme to appreciate the risks, the sentence may be reduced.

General Principle: If the intoxication is voluntary then it is unlikely to represent a valid defence.

DPP v Majewski [1976] 2 All ER 142
Facts: The Defendant took a mixture of drugs and alcohol and subsequently assaulted the landlord in a pub brawl. His conviction was upheld. **Ratio: The Defendant's intoxication was the result of his own voluntary reckless act, said the House of Lords, and the trial judge had rightly directed the jury that they were to ignore it in considering whether he had formed the necessary mens rea in a crime of basic intent. Lord Elwyn-Jones LC said that if a man of his own volition takes a substance which causes him to cast off the restraints of reason and conscience, no wrong is done to him by holding him answerable criminally for any injury he may do while in that condition. His conduct in reducing himself to that condition supplies the evidence of mens rea sufficient for crimes of basic intent. Lord Simon said one of the prime purposes of the criminal law is the protection from certain proscribed conduct, including unprovoked violence, of persons who are pursuing their lawful lives.** **Application:** To allow intoxication as a defence would leave the citizen legally unprotected from unprovoked violence where this was the consequence of drink or drugs having obliterated the capacity of the perpetrator to know what he was doing.

THE DISTINCTION BETWEEN BASIC INTENT AND SPECIFIC INTENT CRIMES

Crimes that are categorized as Specific Intent crimes are those where the only form of *mens rea* available *is* intention- for example- only recklessness was insufficient mens rea to establish the crime. Contrastingly, a crime can be termed as a basic intent where the conviction can be based on the basis of recklessness as to consequences, or where no foresight as to the consequences is required.

The distinction can be better understood with the help of this figure:

Basic Intent Crimes	Specific Intent Crimes
Unlawful Act and Gross Negligence Manslaughter	Murder
Rape and Sexual Touching	Section 18 GBH or Wounding
Assault Occasioning Actual Bodily Harm	Robbery
Section 20 GBH or Wounding	Theft
Assault or Battery	Section 9(1)(a) Burglary with intent to commit an offence under s.(2)
Criminal Damage (or the aggravated offence)where either intention or recklessness isalleged	Criminal damage where it is only alleged that the Defendant intended the damage or intended to endanger life by the damage caused.
	An attempt to commit an offence requiring specific intent.

INTOXICATION AS A DEFENCE

General Principle: Intoxication cannot be used as a defence by a Defendant, whether the crime he has committed is one of specific or basic intent.

R v Morhall [1995] 3 All ER 659
Facts: A habitual glue-sniffer killed another man who nagged him about his habit. The defendant was charged with murder and claimed he had been provoked. **Ratio: Lord Goff said the judge should have directed the jury to take the Defendant's glue-sniffing into account when considering the gravity of the provocation, even though it was discreditable and self-induced (and not necessarily permanent). The question then was whether a sober person with ordinary self-control but otherwise similar to the defendant would have been provoked. The comparison to be made was with an ordinary person,**

rather than with a reasonable person as the term is understood elsewhere. All the relevant circumstances should be taken into account in assessing the gravity of the provocation, but the defendant's reaction should then be compared with that of the ordinary sober person of the same age and sex, with ordinary powers of self-control. **Application:** Dismissing the Defendant's appeal against a conviction for murder, the Court of Appeal said that since the reasonable man did not sniff glue, the Defendant's glue-sniffing was not a relevant factor. The House of Lords disagreed and substituted a conviction for manslaughter.

VOLUNTARY INTOXICATION AND CRIMES OF SPECIFIC INTENT

R v Aidid (Kinse) [2021] EWCA Crim 581

Facts: A was found guilty of murder for having caused V's death by using prolonged aggression after having consumed a large amount of alcohol. On appeal, A admitted that she was guilty of manslaughter and argued that the judge had not properly directed the jury on the impact of alcohol on intent. A argued that the judge had failed to properly advise the jury on the effect of drinking on intent. The court's written instruction to the jury, which was brief but correct, was to the effect of asking, *"Are we sure that the defendant intended the attack to cause really serious bodily harm to [J]?"* **Ratio: The judge then dismissed the appeal. When deciding how to approach the question of the defendant's purpose, if you come to the conclusion that she was under the influence of alcohol, you should take it into consideration; nevertheless, you should also keep in mind that a drunken intent is still intent. He added that the most important point was whether or not A's intoxication and lack of sleep may have had the effect of preventing the prosecution from proving that she had the intention to commit murder. Application:** The court came to the conclusion that this guidance adhered to the authoritative direction that was provided in Sheehan and Moore (per Lane LJ):

"the mere fact that the defendant's mind was affected by drink so that he acted in a way in which he would not have done had he been sober does not assist him

at all, provided that the necessary intent was there, for a drunken intent is nevertheless an intent; secondly, the jury should be instructed to have regard to all the evidence, including the evidence relating to drink, to draw such inferences as they think proper from the evidence, and on that basis to ask themselves whether they feel sure that at the material time the defendant had the requisite intent."

This is a very important piece of information to keep in mind because it indicates that drunkenness may be used as a defence against a crime that requires specific intent only if it was able to prevent the creation of the intention that is required to prove the crime that was committed. In the event that it does not, the position is very clear: "an intent while drunk is still intent."

DIMINISHED RESPONSIBILITY

The Defendant may use diminished responsibility as defence whether he argues that his mental functions were impaired at the time of the crime.

General Principle: Intoxication is no bar to a plea of diminished responsibility as the jury needs to establish whether the defendant was suffering from an abnormality of mental functioning which substantially affected his ability to do one of the things stated in the act.

R v Tandy [1989] 1 All ER 267
Facts: An alcoholic Defendant was charged with the murder of her 11-year-old daughter, but claimed diminished responsibility due to her having drunk a whole bottle of vodka. **Ratio: Drunkenness is not an "abnormality of mind", and only if alcoholism had reached such a state that the brain had been injured, or the drinking was purely involuntary, might a defence of diminished responsibility succeed. If the Defendant simply failed to resist an impulse to drink - even if only the first drink was voluntary - she could not avail herself of this defence. Application:** The Court of Appeal dismissed the Defendant's appeal against a conviction for murder.

General Principle: If the Defendant is suffering from Alcohol Dependency Syndrome (ADS) the jury decides whether his mental responsibility was sufficiently impaired at the time of the killing.

R v Stewart [2009] EWCA Crim 593
Facts: The Defendant was a chronic alcoholic sleeping rough in Marble Arch. He killed a man during a fight. He raised the defence of diminished responsibility. **Ratio: The Court of Appeal gave guidance as to how a judge should direct the jury in cases involving ADS. An evidence of ADS may well assist the jury here. However, it would, depending on the evidence, be open to them to conclude that, notwithstanding the existence of the condition, at the time of the killing, the Defendant was not suffering from an abnormality of mental functioning. If the jury are satisfied that the defendant was suffering from an abnormality, they then need to be satisfied that this arises from a recognized medical condition. If there is clear evidence of ADS, then this requirement is likely to be satisfied. The Court of Appeal suggested: "Without seeking to be prescriptive about considerations relevant to an individual case, the defendant's pattern of drinking in the days leading to the day of the killing, and on the day of the killing itself, and notwithstanding his consumption of alcohol, his ability, if any, to make apparently sensible and rational decisions about ordinary day to day matters at the relevant time, may all bear on the jury's decision whether diminished responsibility is established in the context of this individual defendant's alcohol dependency syndrome." Application:** The jury needs to establish whether the ADS substantially impaired the Defendant's mental responsibility.

SELF- DEFENCE

It is a common law defence. Whether the Defendant causes injury or death to someone with proportional force reasonably used due to the circumstances to protect himself or others, he may be acquitted.

General Principle: If a man under the influence of alcohol and makes a mistake as to the need for self- defence, he cannot rely on that mistake.

R v O'Connor [1991] Crim LR 135
Facts: In a drunken state, the Defendant killed another man in a fight. **Ratio: If the mistake is due to the voluntary intoxication of the Defendant, then the Defendant will not be able to rely on his mistake. A mistaken belief as to the need of self- defence induced by voluntary intoxication is not a valid defence. Application:** The Court of Appeal quashed his conviction for murder and substituted a verdict of manslaughter. The Court claimed that the trial judge should have instructed the jury to consider the Defendant's specific intent or lack of intent in the light of his intoxication, and had failed to do so.

General Principle: The Defendant's belief in consent for offences under the Sexual Offences Act must be reasonable, which it will not be if he makes a drunken mistake.

R v Fotheringham [1989] 88 Cr App R 206
Facts: A man and his wife went out for the evening, leaving a 14-year-old girl babysitting. The wife had told the girl to sleep in the bed. The Defendant came home drunk, got into the bed, and had sex with the girl without her consent, but stopped when his wife came in. The Defendant was charged with rape, but claimed he had mistaken the girl for his consenting wife. **Ratio: A mistake resulting from self-induced intoxication, as regards either the victim's consent or identity, could never be a defence to a charge of rape. Application:** Dismissing his appeal against conviction, the Court of Appeal affirmed his guiltiness for rape.

General Principle: Intoxication can be used as a defence in certain consent cases.

R v Richardson & Irwin [1999] 1 Cr App R 392
Facts: During horseplay following an evening's drinking, two students lifted another over a balcony and dropped him about 12 feet to the ground, causing him serious injuries. **Ratio: At their**

trial for causing grievous bodily harm, the Recorder told the jury they should convict if a sober person in the Defendants' position would have foreseen a risk of injury. Allowing the Defendants' appeal against conviction, Clarke LJ said the question was not what another person would have foreseen but what the Defendants would have foreseen had they been sober.** Application:** In this case, their intoxication was used as a defence.

STATUTORY DEFENCES

General Principle: The Defendant will be able to use this defence even if his belief is due to his voluntary intoxication.

Jaggard v Dickinson [1980] 3 All ER 716
Facts: A woman broke into a house under the drunken mistake that it belonged to a friend. **Ratio: Under certain statutory defences, even if the belief is caused by voluntary intoxication it is considered as a valid defence. Application:** Quashing her conviction for causing criminal damage, The Divisional Court said the Act provided an express defence for anyone who believed the person whom she believed to be the owner would have consented to the damage. Although the defendant's mistake was not a reasonable one, Parliament had provided a defence based on honest belief, and the usual common law rules did not apply.

CONSENT

There are two elements to consent. First, whether the victim consented and second, whether the Defendant believed that the victim consented.

General Principle: The prosecution has to prove that the victim did not consent and the Defendant did not believe in the consent.

R v Donovan [1934] 2 KB 498

Facts: The Defendant paid a prostitute to allow him to cane her, and was subsequently convicted of an assault causing actual bodily harm. **Ratio: So far as the criminal law is concerned, where the act charged is itself unlawful there is no need to prove the absence of consent. There are many acts harmless in themselves, said Swift J, which become unlawful only when done without the consent of the other, but as a general rule (to which there are well established exceptions) it is unlawful for one person to beat another with such violence that bodily harm is a probable consequence, and when such an act is proved the consent of the victim is immaterial. Application:** If serious bodily harm is involved, the consent of the victim is immaterial. The Court of Criminal Appeal quashed the conviction because of misdirection to the jury.

CONSENT AS A DEFENCE FOR OFFENCES AGAINST THE PERSON

General Principle: Consent is available as a defence to assault and battery.

Attorney-General's Reference (No.6 of 1980) [1981] 2 All ER 1057
Facts: Two youths had an argument and decided to settle it by fighting in a public street, and one suffered a bleeding nose. **Ratio: An assailant is not generally guilty of assault where the victim consents, said Lord Lane CJ, but the law makes an exception to this rule where the public interest requires it, and it is not in the public interest for people to try to cause one another bodily harm for no good reason. Minor struggles are another matter, but it is an assault if actual bodily harm is intended or caused. The defence does not extend to assault occasioning actual bodily harm. Application:** At trial on charges of assault, the judge told the jury that there would be no assault if both parties consented and the Defendant used no more than reasonable force; the jury acquitted. On a reference by the Attorney-General, the Court of Appeal said this direction was wrong in law.

General Principle: Consent cannot be regarded as defence for anything greater than a battery.

R v Brown [1993] 2 All ER 75
Facts: A group of middle-aged homosexuals took part in various sado-masochistic activities for their mutual pleasure. All the acts were done with the consent of the "victim", and none of the injuries was serious enough to need hospital treatment. **Ratio: It is not in the public interest, said Lord Lane CJ that people should cause each other actual bodily harm for no good reason, and the satisfying of sado-masochistic libido is not a good reason. The majority in the House of Lords agreed, and said sado-masochistic practices are not in the public interest and should not therefore be added to the list of exceptions. Recent developments in case law have extended the defence of consent to include section 47 which covers actual bodily harm.**

Application: The Defendants were convicted of various offences including malicious wounding and assault.

General Principle: If the Defendant intended only to commit a battery with the consent of the victim, but caused actual bodily harm, then consent is available as a defence.

R v Meachen [2006] EWCA Crim 2414
Facts: The Defendant had consensual sex with the victim which caused her actual bodily harm. **Ratio: The Court of Appeal has expanded the use of consent as a defence and included section 47 ABH in its ambit. If the Defendant intended to commit a battery with the victim's consent but instead committed actual bodily harm, then consent will be available as a defence. Contrastingly, if the Defendant intended to commit actual bodily harm even though the victim consented, consent is not available as a defence (unless it falls under the exceptions discussed later). Application:** This case law expanded the ambit of consent as a defence.

THE EXCEPTIONS

General Principle: Participants of a sport have consented to incidental injuries and will not generally be an offence.

R v Barnes [2005] WLR 910
Facts: During a football match, the Defendant tackled the football very late which caused a serious leg injury to the victim. **Ratio: The jury had to consider the point whether the late tackle had been so late that it could not be regarded as an intuitive reaction or a mistake or misjudgement in the heat of the moment. The Court of Appeal claimed that in organized sports only those situations where the conduct was 'sufficiently grave' should be categorized as criminal. The Court held that , "Whether conduct reached this level depended on all the circumstances which included the type of sport, the level at which it was played, the nature of the act, the degree of force used, the extent of the risk of injury and the state of mind of the defendant. In highly competitive sports**

conduct outside the rules might be expected to occur in the heat of the moment; the fact that such conduct was penalized and even resulted in a warning or a sending off, did not necessarily mean that the threshold level required for it to be regarded as criminal had been reached. Application: The jury had to conclude whether the reaction had been late or violent to be regarded as an instinctive reaction or error in the game.

General Principle: The participants to a game have consented to play the game and have consented to incidental injuries.

R v Jones [1986] 83 Cr App R 375
Facts: The Defendants were playing a game in the school playground in which they threw other boys into the air and caught them. Two such boys suffered a ruptured spleen and a broken arm respectively, and the Defendants were charged with causing grievous bodily harm. The Defendants claimed it was all done in fun, and that the victims had consented. **Ratio: Even if there is no intention to cause injury and the parties consented to incidental injuries during a game, the defence of consent is available. Application:** Quashing their convictions, the Court of Appeal said that the victim's consent (or the Defendant's honest belief in that consent) to rough and undisciplined play could provide a defence as long as there was no intention to cause injury - mere foresight of possible bruising (or even of greater harm) was not sufficient.

General Principle: The participants to a game have consented to play the game and have consented to incidental injuries.

R v Richardson & Irwin [1999] 1 Cr App R 392
Facts: During horseplay following an evening's drinking, two students lifted another over a balcony and dropped him about 12 feet to the ground, causing him serious injuries. **Ratio: At their trial for causing grievous bodily harm, the Recorder told the jury they should convict if a sober person in the Defendant's position would have foreseen a risk of injury. Allowing the Defendant's appeal against conviction, Clarke LJ said the question was not what another person would have foreseen**

but what the Defendants would have foreseen had they been sober. **Application:** This exception has received a lot of criticism.

General Principle: The defence does not extend to cover consent given for sexual gratification.

R v Brown [1993] 2 All ER 75
Facts: A group of middle-aged homosexuals took part in various sado-masochistic activities for their mutual pleasure. All the acts were done with the consent of the "victim", and none of the injuries was serious enough to need hospital treatment. The Defendants were convicted of various offences including malicious wounding and assault, and the convictions were upheld by the Court of Appeal. **Ratio: It is not in the public interest, said Lord Lane CJ that people should cause each other actual bodily harm for no good reason, and the satisfying of sado-masochistic libido is not a good reason. Acts that are against public interest cannot be covered by the defence. Application:** The majority in the House of Lords agreed, and said sado-masochistic practices are not in the public interest and should not therefore be added to the list of exceptions.

General Principle: Consent will be considered as a defence in cases involving tattoos, body piercing and other personal adornment.

R v Wilson [1996] 2 Cr App R 241
Facts: A man was convicted of assault causing actual bodily harm, and conditionally discharged, after branding his initials on his wife's buttocks with a hot knife. The wife had fully consented, but the matter had been reported by her doctor. **Ratio: In cases which involve such decisions between husband and wife, it is not a matter of a criminal investigation. Application:** Allowing the Defendant's appeal, the Court of Appeal said the prosecution had served no useful purpose. There was no evidence that the branding had been any more dangerous or painful than tattooing, and the case was easily distinguishable from those in which real torture had been inflicted.

WHAT AMOUNTS TO CONSENT BY THE VICTIM?

General Principle: Only a deception as to the nature or quality of the act or the accused's identity would vitiate consent.

R v Richardson [1998] 2 Cr App R 200
Facts: A dentist suspended by the General Dental Council continued to treat patients and was subsequently convicted of assault occasioning actual bodily harm. The dentist had not told the victim that she had been suspended, and there was clear evidence that the victim would not have consented to her treating them had they known. **Ratio: The victim might well have a civil claim, but so far as the criminal law is concerned the only mistakes capable of vitiating consent (whether or not induced by fraud) are mistakes as to the nature of the act or as to the identity of the person performing it. Application:** Allowing the Defendant's appeal, Otton LJ said the same principles apply in non-sexual as in sexual assault cases. A deception as to the accused's attributes, status or qualifications would not vitiate consent.

General principle: The consent is vitiated when the victim has been misled or deceived.

R v Tabassum [2000] Times 26/5/00, CA
Facts: A man told several women that he was conducting a breast cancer survey; believing him to be medically qualified they allowed him to feel their breasts. **Ratio: The Defendant's touching of the women's breasts was indecent unless they had consented to that touching, and they had not consented to any touching except for medical purposes. Application:** The Defendant's conviction for indecent assault was affirmed on appeal: although there was no evidence of a sexual motive. Hence, the consent given by the women was vitiated due to deception.

SUMMARY

- The principle of intoxication allows the Defendant to use evidence of his intoxication to prove that he did not form the necessary *mens rea* for the offence.

- Where the Defendant has been involuntarily intoxicated so that he lacks the *mens rea* required to validate the offence, he will be acquitted.

- It is very rare that voluntary intoxication will be use as a valid defence.

- Crimes that are categorized as Specific Intent crimes are those where the only form of *mens rea* available *is* intention.

- Basic intent is proved where the conviction can be based on the basis of recklessness as to consequences, or where no foresight as to the consequences is required.

- The Defendant may use diminished responsibility as defence whether he argues that his mental functions were impaired at the time of the crime.

- Self-defence is valid whether the Defendant causes injury or death to someone with proportional force reasonably used due to the circumstances to protect himself or others.

- There are two elements to consent. First, whether the victim consented and second, whether the Defendant believed that the victim consented. The defence of consent may be subjected to exceptions.

Chapter 10 - Defences of Self-defence & Infancy, Duress & Necessity

INTRODUCTION

This chapter will consider self-defence, infancy, duress and necessity as defences.

SELF- DEFENCE

Self -defence can be used to protect oneself or another, or property from an actual attack or the threat of an imminent attack.

General Principle: The Defendant is entitled to use such force as is reasonable in the circumstances as it appears to him, whether his belief is reasonable or not.

R v Williams (Gladstone) [1987] 3 All ER 411
Facts: A thief who robbed a woman in the street was apprehended by a bystander who caught him and knocked him down. The thief called for help, and a young man (who had not seen the start of the incident) intervened and hit the bystander in order to protect the thief from further beating. **Ratio: At the Defendant's trial on charges of assault causing actual bodily harm, the Recorder said that the Defendant's mistaken belief that the bystander was acting unlawfully would be a defence only if it was reasonable. The Court of Appeal overruled this direction and said that any honest mistake would be sufficient. The reasonableness or unreasonableness of the Defendant's belief, said Lord Lane CJ, is material to the question whether the belief was held by the Defendant at all, but if the belief was in fact held its unreasonableness is irrelevant. The jury should be told that the prosecution has the burden of proving the unlawfulness of the Defendant's actions, and that if the Defendant was labouring under a mistake as to the facts he must be judged according to his mistaken view, whether or not on an objective view that mistake was reasonable.** **Application:** Hence, the Court held that the Defendant's actions

must be judged according to the facts as he honestly believed them to be.

General Principle: If the mistaken belief is due to voluntary intoxication, in this case the Defendant will not be able to rely on his mistake.

R v O'Connor [1991] Crim LR 135
Facts: In a drunken state, the Defendant killed another man in a fight. **Ratio: The question here was whether the crime was a specific intent or basic intent crime. Application:** The Court of Appeal quashed his conviction for murder and substituted a verdict of manslaughter and stated that the trial judge should have instructed the jury to consider the Defendant's specific intent or lack of intent in the light of his intoxication, and had failed to do so.

General Principle: The amount of force used must be reasonable.

R v Owino [1995] Crim LR 743
Facts: A man was convicted of assaulting his wife causing her actual bodily harm, and his appeal was dismissed. **Ratio: The jury must decide if the force used was objectively reasonable in the given circumstances as the defendant subjectively believed them to be. Application:** The Court said that in cases of self-defence based on mistake, a Defendant may use as much force as is objectively reasonable in the circumstances as he subjectively believes them to be. He is not necessarily entitled to use as much force as he believes is reasonable, and to that extent the trial judge's direction to the jury had actually erred in the Defendant's favour.

General Principle: Under English law, there is no duty to retreat.

R v Bird [1985] 2 All ER 513
Facts: During an argument, the victim slapped the Defendant and pushed her back against a wall. The Defendant lunged at the victim with a glass in her hand, injuring him, and was charged

with unlawful wounding. **Ratio: The trial judge told the jury it was necessary that a person claiming to exercise a right of self-defence should demonstrate by her action that she does not want to fight. Allowing the Defendant's appeal, Lord Lane CJ said this went too far: evidence that a Defendant tried to retreat would certainly be powerful evidence that he was neither the aggressor nor seeking revenge, but that was all. Application:** Hence even when the Defendant does not run away it makes a good defence.

General Principle: The Defendant can make the first blow and still rely on the defence. He does not have to wait for the attacker to strike first.

Beckford v R [1987] 3 All ER 425
Facts: A police officer while investigating a report that a man was terrorising his family, shot and killed a man who ran out of the house. **Ratio: Anticipatory self- defence can be justified if the circumstances demand it. Application:** Allowing the Defendant's appeal against his conviction for murder, Lord Griffiths said *obiter* that a man about to be attacked does not have to wait for his assailant to strike the first blow or strike the first shot; circumstances may justify a pre-emptive strike.

General Principle: The defence of self- defence can also be used by an antagonist.

R v Rashford [2005] EWCA Crim 3377
Facts: The Defendant stabbed the victim in the chest after an argument. The Defendant claimed it as an accident. The Defendant with two others then visited the victim "to teach him a lesson". **Ratio: The Court made it clear that self-defence is available to the person who started the fight if the person whom he attacks not only defends himself but goes over to the offensive. Application:** The Court of Appeal opined that self-defence is not automatically precluded in a situation if the Defendant was the initial aggressor and the victim retaliated. The success of the defence would depend on the circumstances of the case. A Defendant can rely on self-defence, if faced with violence

that makes him think he was in immediate danger from which he had no other means of escape (using no more violence than was necessary to protect himself).

General Principle: Self- defence is a complete defence for every crime but if it fails even partially then it fails in its entirety.

R v Clegg [1995] 1 All ER 334
Facts: A soldier at a checkpoint in Northern Ireland shot and killed a teenage "joy-rider" travelling in a car that failed to stop, and was charged with murder. **Ratio: Lord Lloyd said obiter that the general defence that the Defendant was acting in obedience to orders was unknown to English law. Moreover, if the self- defence fails in any way, it will fail in its entirety e.g., if a Defendant uses slightly excessive force, there is no partial defence of self-defence. Application:** This is an all or nothing defence and the appeal was dismissed.

General Principle: Self- defence is a complete defence for every crime but if it fails even partially then it fails in its entirety.

R v Magson [2022] EWCA Crim 1064
The appellant, M, was convicted of the homicide of her companion, V, after a retrial. She struck him in self-defence following a night of heavy drinking, during which M refused to let V into her home. Later, a physical altercation ensued after V kicked open the front door. M wielded a dagger and fatally wounded V, resulting in his death. The judge instructed the jury on the elements of self-defence without reference to the 'householder defence' in sections 76(5A) and (8A) of the Criminal Justice and Immigration Act of 2008 (CJAIA). On appeal, one of M's arguments was that the judge erred in not requesting the jury to consider whether her response was reasonable, given that she believed V to be an intruder in her home. **Ratio: The Court of Appeal ruled, in dismissing the appeal, that the householder defence was inapplicable in cases such as this one, in which a confrontation occurs between two parties who are familiar with each other and there is no evidence that the accused believed the victim was a trespasser at the time of the stabbing. Application:** In fact, the appellant had not argued that she

believed the deceased, who had resided with M for months and had a key to the property, to be a trespasser.

INFANCY

Section 16 of the Children and Young Persons Act 1963 under the Age of 10, are conclusively presumed to be incapable of committing any offences: *'doli incapax'*.

General Principle: The defence of *doli incapax* can never apply to children above the age of 10.

R v T [2008] EWCA Crim 815
Facts: A twelve-year-old defendant was charged with sexual assault. **Ratio: The criminal liability of children aged 10 and above is thus now determined according to the principles relating to *actus reus* and *mens rea* applicable to adults.** **Application:** The judge ruled that the defence of *doli incapax* was not open to the Defendant. The Defendant appealed this on the grounds that only the presumption of *'doli incapax'* had been abolished but not the idea itself. The appeal was dismissed.

DURESS

When a person commits an act which would normally be a criminal act, but he committed it as a result of a serious threat made against him he can use this as a defence.

General Principle: The Defendant must prove that he acted under a serious threat of death or personal injury.

R v Graham [1982] 1 All ER 801
Facts: A homosexual man lived with his wife and another homosexual man. The two men together killed the wife and were charged with murder. The husband claimed that he acted under the other man's duress was not accepted by the jury and he was charged with murder. The husband appealed on the grounds that

the judge had directed the jury that his subjective fear was not enough, and that his acts must have been those of a reasonable man. **Ratio: The threat must be one of death or serious personal injury. Application:** The Court of Appeal dismissed the appeal and upheld his conviction. The proper test, said Lord Lane CJ, was to ask whether the husband was impelled to act as he did because (as a result of what he reasonably believed the other man to have said or done) he had good cause to fear that if he did not so act then the other man would kill him or do him serious physical injury; and if so, whether a sober person of reasonable firmness, but sharing the defendant's other characteristics, would have acted similarly in those circumstances. The fact that the Defendant's will to resist might have been overborne by drink or drugs would not be relevant.

General Principle: The defence of 'duress' cannot be used in defence to a murder charge.

R v Howe [1987] 1 All ER 771
Facts: The Defendant took part with others in two separate murders, and on a third occasion the intended victim escaped. The defendant's claim to have acted under duress was left to the jury on two of the three counts, but the defendant was convicted on all three, and appealed. **Ratio: The Defendant can never use 'duress' as a defence for murder. Application:** The House of Lords reviewed the authorities, and then exercised its power under the 1966 Practice Statement to depart from the norm. No participant (whether principal or accessory) can claim duress in defence to a murder charge. The justification for this decision is that the law should deny a man the right to take an innocent life even at the price of his own (per Lord Griffiths), but should rather set a standard of heroism and self-sacrifice which ordinary men and women should be expected to observe (per Lord Hailsham).

General principle: The defence of 'duress' cannot be used in defence to an attempted murder charge either.

R v Gotts [1992] 1 All ER 833

Facts: The defendant's father ordered him to kill his mother and threatened to shoot him if he did not do so. The Defendant therefore stabbed his mother and injured her seriously, but did not actually kill her. **Ratio: The defence of duress is not available in cases of attempted murder and murder. The main difference between murder and attempted murder is the pure chance that the victim dies or lives, and attempted murder may be morally worse in requiring an intention to cause death and no less. Application:** He was charged with attempted murder, and claimed duress as a defence, saying he had done it only because his own life was in danger, but the trial judge refused to allow this defence to go to the jury. Dismissing the Defendant's appeal and applying a dictum of Lord Griffiths in *Howe*, the House decided that duress is not available to a person charged with attempted murder (nor, per Lord Lowry, with "most kinds of treason").

General Principle: If the Defendant voluntarily becomes or remains associated with people engaged in a criminal activity in a situation where he knows or ought to reasonably know that he may be subject to compulsion, in such a case the defence of duress will not be available.

R v Hasan [2005] UKHL 22
Facts: The Defendant armed with a knife forced his way into a house with an intention to steal the contents of a safe. At the trial, he raised the defence of duress, claiming that one person Sullivan, a person with a reputation of violence, had threatened to harm the Defendant and his family unless he carried out the burglary in question. The Defendant had an existing association with Sullivan. **Ratio: The House of the Lords restored the defendant's conviction. The rationale for the voluntary exposure exception is that the defendant volunteers for the risk; but this cannot be said for someone who joins a violent organisation unaware of the risk. The merely negligent do not "buy into", or "court", their fate. "The policy of the law must be to discourage association with known criminals," asserts Lord Bingham. Application:** The House is clearly concerned by the intertwined growth of the duress defence and the modern

prevalence of organised crime and the law cannot be used to shield criminals.

General Principle: The defence is allowed only when the threat of death or serious injury was the sole reason behind the Defendant committing the crime

R v Valderrama-Vega [1985] Crim LR 220
Facts: The Defendant was charged with importing prohibited drugs, and claimed duress; he claimed that the Colombian drug dealers had threatened to kill or injure the Defendant and his family if he did not comply. He was also under financial pressure and had been threatened with disclosure of his homosexuality. **Ratio: Cumulative effect of all the threats could be considered provided that the Defendant would not have acted had it not been for the threat of death or serious injury. Application:** Allowing his appeal, the Court of Appeal said the threat to expose the Defendant to criminal charges was not itself a defence (though it could be considered in mitigation of sentence), but that so long as the threats of physical violence were *sine qua non* to the Defendant's decision, the other factors too could be taken into account.

General Principle: There must be a connection between the threat and the crime.

R v Cole [1994] Crim LR 582
Facts: A man was charged with robbery at several building societies, and claimed he owed money to moneylenders who had threatened to harm to him and his girlfriend if he did not repay it. **Ratio: The threat must specify the offence that is carried out. Application:** The trial judge ruled this could not constitute duress; the Defendant then pled guilty and subsequently appealed. Dismissing his appeal, the Court of Appeal said the defence of duress by threats required that the threatened should have specified the offence to be carried out.

General Principle: An honestly held belief was sufficient, even if that belief was unreasonable.

R v Martin [1989] 1 All ER 652

Facts: The defendant was charged with driving while disqualified; his defence was that his stepson was late for work and at risk of losing his job, and the defendant's wife had threatened to kill herself if the defendant did not take the boy to work. **Ratio: Allowing the defendant's appeal against conviction, Simon Brown J said English Law does recognise a limited defence of necessity: most often it arises as duress, but duress can result from circumstances rather than from the threats of others. The defence is available only if the defendant can objectively be said to have acted reasonably and proportionately to avoid a threat of death or serious injury, and it is then for the jury to say whether on the basis of the defendant's reasonable belief he had good cause to fear death or serious physical injury to himself or another, and whether a sober person of reasonable firmness, sharing the defendant's other characteristics, would have responded to the situation as the defendant did. The Court doubted whether the jury would have accepted the defendant's story (particularly since there was another driver in the house), but they should have been allowed to consider it. Application:** Defence of duress of circumstances is possible but the defendant has to prove that the belief that there would be serious physical injury to him or another must be immediate.

General Principle: The question to consider is whether a sober person of reasonable firmness, sharing the characteristics of the defendant, would have done what the defendant did.

R v Bowen [1997] 1 WLR 372

Facts: The defendant was charged with obtaining services (viz, credit) by deception, and pled duress: he had been threatened that his home would be petrol-bombed if he did not provide various electrical goods.

Ratio: Dismissing his appeal against conviction, the Court of Appeal said it was not necessary for the jury to take into account the defendant's low intelligence (short of mental impairment) when considering the effect of the threats on a

reasonable person. Stuart-Smith LJ suggested the principles could be summarised as follows:

"[1] The defendant's vulnerability or timidity are not to be ascribed to the reasonable person for the purposes of the objective test. [2] The Defendant may be in a category of persons that the jury might think were less able than others to resist threats: for example, young people, possibly women (though many women might disagree), pregnant women afraid for their unborn child, persons with physical disabilities inhibiting their self-protection, or persons with a recognised psychiatric disorder supported by medical evidence. [3] Characteristics relevant in provocation because they related to the nature of the provocation (for example, the defendant's homosexuality) would not necessarily be relevant in duress, and characteristics due to self-abuse (such as drunkenness) can never be relevant."

Application: Low IQ has been excluded from the list of characteristics that the court will have regard to.

General Principle: Where the defendant had an opportunity to avoid the consequences of the threat the defence of duress is unlikely to succeed.

R v Abdul-Hussain & others (1999) Times 26/1/99
Facts: Six Shi'ite Muslims living in Iraq hijacked an airplane bound for Jordan and forced it to fly to Britain, where they surrendered peacefully after a few hours.
Ratio: At their trial they claimed they were in fear of their lives as opponents of the existing Iraqi regime, but the judge said this threat was not imminent at the time of the hijacking and refused to put this defence to the jury. Allowing the defendant's appeal, Rose LJ said the defence of duress was available in circumstances such as these: they did not have to wait for the knock on the door.
Application: A failure to take an opportunity to avoid the consequences will not always prevent the defence from operating.

NECESSITY

General Principle: The defence of necessity is made available when the defendant acts in a certain way because a failure to act will result in a greater danger.

R v Bourne [1938] 3 All ER 615
Facts: A 14-year-old girl was pregnant as the result of rape, and a doctor carried out an abortion to protect the girl from serious injury. **Ratio: The judge suggested that the word "unlawfully" in Section 58 of the Offences Against the Person Act 1861 might be taken to exclude the case in which the act was done solely to preserve the life of the expectant mother; that, he said, had long been the common law position. Moreover, if the risk to the woman's health is sufficiently grave, an act done to preserve her health may be regarded as being to preserve her life even though she may not be in imminent danger of death. The jury found the Defendant not guilty. Application:** The court said the action had been justified by the danger to life.

General Principle: The defence of necessity has been allowed in many medical cases where what is done is considered to be in the best interests of the 'victim'.

F v West Berkshire Health Authority [1989] 2 All ER 545
Facts: A 36-year-old woman with a mental age of 5 had formed a close relationship with a male patient in the same hospital. Doctors agreed that the psychological effects of pregnancy would be seriously damaging to her, and (since she could not cope with normal methods of contraception) sought a declaration that they would be acting lawfully in sterilising the woman without obtaining her consent, which she was mentally incapable of giving. **Ratio: Lord Brandon said that where an adult patient is unable to give or refuse consent - for example, because he is unconscious or mentally disabled, the doctor has a right - perhaps even a duty - to give treatment that is in the patient's best interests, to save his life or to prevent deterioration or ensure improvement in his physical or mental health. Lord Goff agreed, and said obiter that a man who seizes another and forcibly drags him from the path of an oncoming vehicle, thereby saving him from injury or even death, commits no**

wrong. Application: In certain medical cases, the defence of necessity has been invoked when the adult patient is unable to give or refuse consent.

DURESS OF CIRCUMSTANCES

A person acts under duress of circumstances if he does so only to avoid death or serious personal injury (to himself or another), perhaps caused by something other than a direct threat by a third party.

General Principle: Duress of circumstances applies to road traffic offences.

R v Willer (1986) 83 Cr App R 225
Facts: The defendant was charged with reckless driving after driving at about 10 mph through a pedestrian precinct to escape from a gang threatening violence to him and his passengers, and pled necessity. **Ratio: In road traffic offences, the courts began to recognise a defence of necessity, which they called duress of circumstances. Application:** The Assistant Recorder said this defence did not exist, and the defendant changed his plea to guilty, but then appealed. The Court of Appeal doubted whether the defendant's actions had in fact been reckless, but said duress should in any case have been left to the jury. This was not the usual sort of duress - the gang had not told the defendant to drive on the pavement - but duress of circumstances could be used even where necessity could not.

General Principle: This defence can equally arise from other objective dangers threatening the accused or others and is conveniently called 'duress of circumstances'.

R v Martin [1989] 1 All ER 652
Facts: The Defendant was charged with driving while disqualified; his defence was that his stepson was late for work and at risk of losing his job, and the Defendant's wife had threatened to kill herself if the Defendant did not take the boy to work. **Ratio: The accused must be acting reasonably and**

proportionately in order to avoid a threat of death or serious personal injury. Application: Allowing the Defendant's appeal against conviction, Simon Brown J said English Law does recognise a limited defence of necessity: most often it arises as duress, but duress can result from circumstances rather than from the threats of others. The defence is available only if the Defendant can objectively be said to have acted reasonably and proportionately to avoid a threat of death or serious injury, and it is then for the jury to say whether on the basis of the Defendant's reasonable belief he had good cause to fear death or serious physical injury to himself or another, and whether a sober person of reasonable firmness, sharing the defendant's other characteristics, would have responded to the situation as the Defendant did. The Court doubted whether the jury would have accepted the Defendant's story (particularly since there was another driver in the house), but they should have been allowed to consider it.

General Principle: The defence would be available where the accused reasonably believed that his action was necessary to prevent death or serious personal injury to himself or another and he had (objectively) acted reasonably and proportionately with respect to the threat.

R v Pommell [1995] 2 Cr App R 607

Facts: Police searching the Defendant's house at about 8 am one morning found him lying in bed with a loaded gun in his hand. His defence was that someone had come to see him during the night, carrying the gun with which he planned to kill someone. The Defendant persuaded the visitor to give him the gun and the visitor left the Defendant then decided to give the gun to the police in the morning. **Ratio: Kennedy LJ said the defence of duress of circumstances was available in crimes other than road traffic offences - in fact, in any offence other than murder, attempted murder, and some form of treason. A person committing an offence under duress of circumstances must desist from doing so as soon as he reasonably can, and it should have been left to the jury to decide whether the delay of some seven hours between the defendant's acquiring the gun and the arrival of the police robbed him of the defence. Application:** Allowing the Defendant's appeal against his conviction for possessing a firearm, and ordering a new trial, the court said that the defence of duress of circumstances was made available for offences beyond traffic offences.

SUMMARY

- Self-defence can be used to protect oneself or another, or property from an actual attack or the threat of an imminent attack.

- The defence of necessity is made available when the Defendant acts in a certain way because a failure to act will result in a greater danger.

- When a person commits an act which would normally be a criminal act, but he committed it as a result of a serious threat made against him he can use duress as a defence.

Chapter 11 - Inchoate Offences: Conspiracy & Attempt

INTRODUCTION

An inchoate offence is an offence where the Defendant has taken steps towards the commission of a crime. Even if the Defendant did not complete the full offence, his conduct reaches such a stage in its commission that a punishment is justified. The main inchoate offences are:

- Encouraging or assisting crime
- Conspiracy
- Attempt

ENCOURAGING OR ASSISTING CRIME

Under this category three potential new offences have been introduced by Part 2 of the Serious Crime Act 2007:

- **Section 44(1)** - intentionally encouraging or assisting an offence

- **Section 45** - encouraging or assisting an offence believing it will be committed

- **Section 46(1)** - encouraging or assisting offences believing one or more will be committed.

General Principle: Whether the Defendant encourages illegal activities (even via social media), he will be found guilty.

R v Blackshaw; Sutcliffe [2011] EWCA Crim 2312
Facts: Blackshaw created a public event on Facebook where he called participants to meet with the purpose to encourage riot, burglary and criminal damage. Sutcliff created a Facebook page inviting contacts and the public to a riot. They both were charged under Section 46 of the Serious Crime Act 2007. **Ratio: The Defendant's words used on the Facebook pages and by his own**

confession were aimed to encourage illegal activity. Application: The Defendants were sentenced to four years imprisonment.

DEFENCE OF ACTING REASONABLY

According to **Section 50** of the Serious Crime Act 2007 anyone charged under **Sections 44-46** may rely on two potential defences:

- **Section 50(1)** - The Defendant needs to prove that he knew of the existence of certain circumstances and that it was reasonable for him to act as he did in those circumstances.

- **Section 50(2)** - The Defendant needs to prove that he believed that certain circumstances existed, that his belief was reasonable and that it was reasonable for him to act as he did in the circumstances as he believed them to be.

STATUTORY CONSPIRACY

The Defendant agrees with someone to commit an offence. It is not required that the Defendant actually put the offence into place. The Defendant will be guilty as long as he has planned to commit it with the required *mens rea*.

Section 1(1) Criminal Law Act 1977:

Subject to the following provisions of this part of the Act, if a person agrees with any other person or persons that a course of conduct shall be pursued which, if the agreement is carried out in accordance with their intentions, either - (a) will necessarily amount to or involve the commission of any offence, or (b) would do so but for the existence of facts which render the commission of the offence or any of the offences impossible, he is guilty of conspiracy to commit the offence or offences in question he is guilty of conspiracy to commit the offence or offences in question.

ACTUS REUS

By looking at **Section 1(1)** of the Criminal Law Act 1977, the actus reus elements are:

- Presence of an agreement

- Between two or more parties

- To do something

- That amounts to a criminal offence

General Principle: The agreement has to be between two or more people and the offence is complete as soon as the parties agree and only terminates on completion by performance, abandonment or frustration.

R v Walker [1962] Crim LR 458
Facts: A man took part in discussions of a possible payroll robbery, but withdrew at an early stage. **Ratio: To establish the offence of conspiracy the presence of an 'agreement' between the parties is essential. Application:** His conviction for conspiracy was quashed because there was no evidence that the discussion had gone any further than mere negotiation, and conspiracy requires at least a measure of agreement.

General Principle: A conspiracy requires the presence of a common unlawful purpose or design between the parties.

R v Shillam [2013] EWCA Crim 160
Facts: The Defendant and two co-accused were charged with conspiracy to supply cocaine. X was the central character. The Defendant and Y were regular purchasers of cocaine from X. The Defendant stopped beside X's car. Shortly afterwards the police stopped the van finding cocaine inside. The Defendant's telephone showed messages of people asking to buy cociane and several phone contact with X. At trial the judge directed the jury to conviction. The Defendant appealed. **Ratio: The prosecution always had to consider carefully how to formulate a conspiracy charge and whether a substantive offence would be**

more appropriate. Conspiracy requires a single joint design between the conspirators. Application: Since it could not be proven that the parties shared a common purpose or design, the appeal was allowed.

CERTAIN PERSONS DO NOT FALL UNDER THE AMBIT OF CONSPIRACY

There are some limitations on who can be guilty of conspiracy to commit an offence.

Section 2(2): Criminal Law Act 1977:

a) An accused cannot conspire with a person who is his spouse at the time of the agreement

b) An accused cannot conspire with a child under 10 years old) An accused cannot conspire with an intended victim of the crime.

MENS REA

The mens rea of conspiracy is intention. The Defendant must:

- intend to enter into the agreement;
- intend that the agreement be carried out; and
- intend or know as to the circumstances of the offence.

General Principle: To establish *mens rea* of the crime it is enough for the prosecution to prove that the Defendant had agreed on a course of conduct which he knew would involve the commission of an offence and the proof that he intended that it be committed was not necessary.

R v Anderson [1986] AC 27
Facts: The Defendant was involved in a conspiracy to escape from prison. The Defendant agreed to take part in it by providing the necessary equipment to cut the bars on the cells. He argued that he never intended for the plan to be carried out and that he did not believe that it could ever succeed. **Ratio: Intention to agree that the offence be committed is not necessary. But this**

judgment has become controversial after various contrary judgments by the Courts. Application: The House of Lords disagreed and Lord Bridge said: "Beyond the mere fact of agreement, the necessary *mens rea* of the crime is, in my opinion, established if, and only if, it is shown that the accused, when he entered into the agreement, intended to play some part in the agreed course of conduct in furtherance of the criminal purpose which the agreed course of conduct was intended to achieve. Nothing less will suffice; nothing more is required."

General Principle: It is the intention to carry out the crime that constitutes the necessary *mens rea* for the offence.

R v Edwards[1991] Crim LR 45
Facts: The Defendant agreed to supply amphetamine, but it may have been the case that he did not intent to carry out his part in the agreement. **Ratio: It was held that the judge rightly directly the jury that the Defendant could not be convicted of conspiracy to supply amphetamine unless he intended to carry out the agreement to do so. Application:** This judgment digressed from Anderson.

For now, Anderson represents the law; it is unlikely that it would be followed by a future House of Lords as it raises a lot of questions.

ATTEMPT

Whether the Defendant has taken sufficient steps for the offence to be committed, he will be guilty of attempt.

Section 1 of Criminal Attempts Act 1981:

(1) If, with intent to commit an offence to which this section applies, a person does an act which is more than merely preparatory to the commission of an offence, he is guilty of an attempt to commit that offence. (2) A person may be guilty of an attempt to commit an offence to which this section applies even though the facts are such that the commission of the offence is

impossible. (3) In any case where: (a) apart from this subsection a person's intention would not be regarded as having amounted to an intent to commit an offence; but (b) if the facts of the case had been as he believed them to be, his intention would be so regarded. Then, for the purposes of subsection (1) above, he shall be regarded as having had intent to commit that offence.

ACTUS REUS

General Principle: The act must be more than merely preparatory and this is a question of fact which is to be decided by the jury.

R v Gullefer [1990] 3 All ER 882
Facts: A man placed a bet on a certain greyhound. Seeing his dog was losing, the Defendant tried to interfere with the race in the hope that it would be declared void and all bets consequently returned. **Ratio: The Defendant's acts have to reach a stage which goes beyond mere preparation. Application:** The Court of Appeal quashed his conviction for attempting to steal his stake money from the bookmaker, and said that as a matter of law he had not done enough for the case to go to the jury. His acts were merely preparatory, and he had not yet embarked on the crime proper.

General principle: The question whether the act was more than preparatory is to be decided by the jury.

R v Jones [1990] 3 All ER 886
Facts: The Defendant pointed a shotgun at his intended victim, and would have had to do at least three more acts (remove the safety catch, put his finger on the trigger, and pull the trigger) in order to shoot. He was stopped before he could go any further, but was charged with attempted murder. **Ratio: An attempt begins when the merely preparatory acts come to an end and the Defendant embarks on the crime proper or the actual commission of the offence. Application:** His conviction was upheld by the Court of Appeal: Taylor LJ declined to apply the

"last act" test and said the only question was whether the defendant's acts were "more than merely preparatory".

General principle: If the acts are merely preparatory and have not reached beyond that stage the courts generally acquit the defendant.

R v Campbell (1991) 93 Cr App R 350
Facts: A man in disguise, carrying a gun and a threatening note, was stopped just outside the door of the post office he had planned to rob. **Ratio: The Defendant was stopped before he could have embarked on the actual commission of the offence. Application:** The Court of Appeal quashed his conviction for attempted robbery, saying his acts could be regarded as merely preparatory until he entered the building. Watkins LJ endorsed the statement of Taylor LJ in Jones above; judges should stick to the definition of an attempt in the Act, he said, and there was no need to refer to earlier common law cases.

General Principle: It is a question of fact whether the Defendant's acts have reached beyond the stage of mere preparation.

R v Tosti [1997] Crim LR 746
Facts: The Defendants were charged with attempted burglary. They had been seen around midnight, examining the padlock on a barn door, but ran off when they realised they were being watched. Their cars were parked in a lay-by nearby and hidden in a hedge between the cars and the barn was an oxy-acetylene cutting set. **Ratio: Whether the Defendants' acts are more than merely preparatory, he must be convicted. Application:** The jury in this case found that examining the padlock and running away when the Defendant thought that they were being watched was enough to term their acts as beyond preparatory.

MENS REA

General Principle: The accused must intend to bring about the consequences required for the full offence.

R v Walker &Hayles [1990] 90 Cr App R 226

Facts: The Defendants threw their victim from a third floor balcony. **Ratio: An intention to bring out the consequences of the offence is enough to establish mens rea. Application:** At their trial for attempted murder the trial judge directed the jury that they could infer intention if there was a high degree of probability that the victim would be killed and if the defendants knew "quite well that in doing that there was a high degree of probability" that the victim would be killed. The defendants appealed that the judge was confusing 'an intention to kill' with 'foresight of death'. The Court of Appeal rejected the appeal.

General Principle: In case of sexual offences, when what is missing from the full offence is the sexual act, for an attempt it is necessary to show an intention to do the sexual act, but only lack of reasonable belief in consent.

Attorney-General's Reference (No.1 of 1992) [1993] 2 All ER 190

Facts: Following the acquittal (on the judge's direction) of a man who had undressed and indecently assaulted a young woman with the intention of raping her, the Court of Appeal were asked to say whether acts prior to an attempt at penetration could be regarded as more than merely preparatory. **Ratio:** In sexual offences, to prove an attempt the intention to commit the act needs to be established. **Application:** They ruled that attempted penetration was not essential, and that so long as there was evidence of intent it was enough to prove acts which the jury could properly infer were more than merely preparatory.

IMPOSSIBILITY

Under Sections 44-46 of the Serious Crime Act 2007 the provision states that the Defendant's conduct must be capable of encouraging or committing the offence. Nevertheless, impossibility cannot be use as a defence.

General Principle: Impossibility in fact is no longer a defence.

Anderton v Ryan [1985] 2 All ER 355

Facts: A woman bought a video recorder in a pub for £110, believing it to be stolen, but there was no evidence to show that it had in fact been stolen and the Defendant was charged with attempting to handle stolen goods. **Ratio: Where a Defendant sets out to commit a crime, which is in fact impossible to commit, it will not be a defence if the Defendant had the intention to commit the crime in the first place. Application:** The judges dismissed the charge but the Divisional Court allowed the prosecution's appeal by way of case stated. On appeal to the House of Lords, the magistrates' decision was restored: the wording of the section, said Lord Roskill, does not compel the conclusion that an erroneous belief in the existence of facts which, if true, would have made the act a crime makes the defendant guilty of an attempt to commit that crime.

General Principle: Impossibility in committing an offence which the defendant clearly intended to commit in the first place cannot be used as a defence.

R v Shivpuri [1986] 2 All ER 334

Facts: The Defendant was arrested entering the country, carrying with him a package which he believed contained either heroin or cannabis, but was in fact ground dried cabbage and quite harmless. The Defendant was charged with attempting to import a prohibited drug, and his appeal was dismissed by the Court of Appeal. **Ratio: Impossibility in carrying out the act is not a valid defence. Application:** The House of Lords stated that the Defendant had clearly intended to commit an offence, and had done an act (bringing in the package) which had the facts been as he believed them to be (that the package contained drugs) would have been more than merely preparatory to that offence; his conviction should therefore be upheld.

SUMMARY

- Inchoate offences enable offenders to be convicted if their conduct reaches such a stage that criminalisation is justified in order to protect society.

- There are three types of inchoate offences: encouraging or assisting crime, statutory conspiracy and attempt.

- Encouraging or assisting crime is regulated under Sections 44-46 of the Serious Crime Act 2007.

- The Defendant may rely on Section 50 that gives the chance to prove reasonableness of the Defendant's action.

- Whether the Defendant agrees with someone to commit an offence with the required *mens rea*, he will be guilty of conspiracy.

- By committing sufficient steps in order to have a full offence, the Defendant will still be guilty.

Chapter 12 - Criminal Damage

INTRODUCTION

This chapter will cover all the aspects of Criminal Damage. Two are the main offences created by the Criminal Damage Act 1971: simple criminal damage and aggravated criminal damage.

CRIMINAL DAMAGE

Criminal Damage is defined under **Section 1(1)** of the Criminal Damage Act 1971:

A person who without lawful excuse damages or destroys any property belonging to another intending to destroy or damage any such property or being reckless as to whether any such property would be destroyed or damaged shall be guilty of an offence.

This offence carries a maximum sentence of 10 years.

ACTUS REUS

The *actus reus* of the offence requires the following elements:

- the Defendant must have destroyed or damaged
- a property belonging to another

General Principle: The damage to property must be more than trivial or nominal.

A (a juvenile) v R [1978] Crim LR 689
Facts: A youth spat on a policeman's raincoat, and was charged with causing criminal damage. **Ratio: In order to have criminal damage the property must be rendered imperfect or inoperable. Application:** Acquitting him in the Crown Court, the judge said spitting on a police raincoat does not cause damage, since it can easily be wiped off. But obiter, spitting on a satin wedding dress might have been a different matter.

General Principle: Whether a property in question is damaged or not is a question of fact and degree.

Roe v Kingerlee [1986] Crim LR 735
Facts: A man smeared graffiti in mud on the walls of a police cell, and was charged with criminal damage. **Ratio: It is a matter of fact and degree, they said, and it is for the justices applying their common sense to decide whether what occurred was damage or not. Application:** The Court has discretion to decide whether there has been criminal damage. The Divisional Court held that this could amount to criminal damage. Whether or not the damage was criminal it was a matter of fact.

General Principle: If the damage can be easily overcome then it will not be 'criminal damage'.

Hardman v Chief Constable of Avon & Somerset [1986] Crim LR 330
Facts: Protestors painted the outlines of bodies on the pavement in Broadmead as part of an anti-nuclear demonstration. **Ratio: The Court also held that the damage need not to be permanent. Application:** Although the paint could be removed with high-pressure hoses, the defendants were found guilty of causing criminal damage because of the trouble and expense of removal.

General Principle: The property that is destroyed or damaged must be tangible.

R v Whiteley [1991] 93 Cr App R 25, CA
Facts: A computer "hacker" gained unauthorised access to a computer network operated by a number of universities. He created and deleted files, changed other users' passwords, and deleted files that would enable his own activities to be traced. He was charged with causing criminal damage to the magnetic disks on which the computer data were stored. **Ratio: A clear distinction had been established between tangible property and tangible damage: the property must be tangible and the damage can also be intangible. Application:** Upholding his

conviction, the Court of Appeal said what was necessary was that tangible property should be damaged or destroyed, not that the damage itself should be tangible. Here tangible property (the magnetic particles on the discs affected) was altered in such a way as to make it less useful to its owner, and that was enough.

MENS REA

Intending to destroy or damage any such property or being reckless as to whether any such property would be destroyed.

General Principle: The *mens rea* for basic criminal damage is the intention or recklessness asto the destruction or damage of property belonging to another.

R v Caldwell [1981] 1 All ER 961
Facts: An ex-employee had a grievance against the owner of a hotel, and set fire to the hotel in revenge. The fire was discovered before it did any serious damage, but there were ten guests in the hotel at the time and Caldwell was charged with aggravated criminal damage "being reckless as to the danger to life". His defence was that he was drunk and had not even considered whether lives might be endangered. **Ratio: The definition of recklessness used by the court is the one set out in clause 18 of the Draft Criminal Code 1989: 'A person acts recklessly with respect to (I) a circumstance when he is aware of a risk, (II) a result when he is aware of a risk that it will occur and it is in the circumstances known to him, unreasonable to take the risk. Application: The House of Lords upheld his conviction, and said it was enough that that the Defendant had given no thought to a risk that was obvious to any reasonable person.**

General Principle: It must also be proved that the Defendant knew or was reckless as to whether the property belonged to another.

R v Smith [1974] 1 All ER 632
Facts: A tenant with his landlord's consent, installed in his flat some electrical wiring for stereo equipment, and covered it over

with ceiling and wall panels and floor boards. When he surrendered his lease, he tore away the panels (which as a matter of land law had now become the landlord's property) to remove the wiring, and was charged with criminal damage. **Ratio: Where the Defendant honestly believed the property was his own he lacked the necessary *mens rea* with regard to the circumstances. No offence is committed under this section if a person destroys or causes damage to property belonging to another if he does so in the honest though mistaken belief that the property is his own. Application:** The court allowed the appeal and quashed his conviction.

General Principle: A mistake due to voluntary intoxication does not vitiate the defence under Section 5(2)(a) of the Criminal Damage Act.

Jaggard v Dickinson [1980] 3 All ER 716
Facts: A woman was drunk, and mistook a house for one that belonged to her friend with whom she was living. She believed (correctly) that her friend would not object to her breaking in, but the true owner did object, and the woman was convicted of causing criminal damage. **Ratio: Even if the Defendant is under the influence of alcohol caused by voluntary consumption this defence will be available to him. Application:** The Divisional Court allowed her appeal: the wording of Section 5(3) was sufficiently clear to override the common law rule that a drunken mistake is no defence, and the defendant's honest (but drunken) mistake was therefore a lawful excuse.

General Principle: If the Defendant honestly believes that the owner of the property has or would have consented to the damage to property, the Defendant's *motive* for causing the damage is irrelevant.

R v Denton [1982] 1 All ER 65
Facts: A man was employed at a certain factory, and his employer asked him to burn down the factory so that (the employer) could make a fraudulent insurance claim. The Defendant complied and was convicted of arson, the trial judge having ruled that the

unlawful purpose deprived the Defendant of any lawful excuse. **Ratio: The consent of the owner for the damage is enough to constitute a defence. Application:** The Court of Appeal quashed the conviction: it is not unlawful for a man to set fire to his own property, and a fraudulent intent does not make it so: Denton had a good defence under Section 5(2)(a).

General Principle: A belief, however powerful, genuine and honestly held that God had given consent was not a lawful excuse under the domestic law of England.

Blake v DPP [1993] Crim LR 586
Facts: A minister took part in a protest against the Gulf War and painted a biblical quotation on a pillar outside the Houses of Parliament. He was charged with causing criminal damage, and the Divisional Court upheld his conviction. **Ratio: The will of God cannot be used as a defence for the charge of criminal damage. Application**: His claim that he was doing the will of God and that God was a fortiori the person entitled to consent was not a defence that could be recognised by the law.

REQUIREMENTS OF SECTION 5(2)(b)

This section comes into operation when the Defendant acts to protect his/hers or another's property.

General Principle: A child does not constitute 'property' under this section.

R v Baker & Wilkins [1997] Crim LR 497
Facts: The Defendant and her lover broke down the door of a house where they believed the defendant's daughter was being held, in order to rescue the child. **Ratio: Brooke LJ said a child is not "property" so the Defendants could not avail themselves of the defence in Section 5(2)(b) of the Act. Application:** Reluctantly affirming their conviction for causing criminal damage, the court pointed out that the Act should be amended to include the protection of persons as well as property.

General Principle: The accused must believe that the property was in immediate need of protection.

Johnson v DPP [1994] Crim LR 673
Facts: Johnson, a squatter in a council house, damaged a door while attempting to fit locks in the house. Johnson was charged with criminal damage and raised the Section 5(2)(b) defence on the grounds that there had been a lot of theft in the area, and that he had therefore acted to protect his property. **Ratio: There is a subjective test where the Defendant needs to establish that the property was in an immediate need of protection. Application:** The Queen's Bench Division upheld his conviction on the grounds that he did not believe his property was in *immediate* need of protection.

General Principle: The accused must believe that the means of protection adopted are reasonable and the damage caused by the accused must be capable of protecting the property.

R v Hunt [1977] Crim LR 740
Facts: The Defendant started a fire in his bedroom in a deserted part of the block in order to check the adequacy of the fire alarm in a block of flats. He then pressed the fire alarm which did not work so he called the fire brigade. **Ratio: The Court held that it was not sufficient that the accused *intended* to prevent further damage to property but also required that the act be objectively *capable* of protecting the property from damage. Application:** The Court of Appeal, rejecting the defence under Section 5(2)(b), introduced an *objective* element into the defence. If the Defendant was trying to protect his property, his actions had to be capable of saving the property.

AGGRAVATED CRIMINAL DAMAGE

The offence represents the aggravated form of simple criminal damage. The maximum sentence is life imprisonment.

Section 1(2) of the 1971 Act provides:

A person who without lawful excuse destroys of damages any property, whether belonging to himself or another; (a) intending to destroy or damage any property or being reckless as whether any property would be destroyed or damaged; and (b) intending by the destruction or damage to endanger life of another or being reckless as to whether the life of another would be thereby endangered; shall be guilty of an offence.

ACTUS REUS

The actus reus elements are the same as per simple criminal damage. The only difference is that aggravated criminal damage requires that some property be damaged, but it does not require that the property belong to another. The property may also belong to the Defendant.

General Principle: As a matter of *actus reus*, it is irrelevant whether the life of another was actually endangered.

R v Sangha [1988] 2 All ER 385
Facts: A man set fire to a mattress and two armchairs in an empty flat. He was charged with aggravated arson being reckless as to the danger to the lives of people in the other flats, though in fact (unknown to the Defendant) the way in which the building was constructed meant there was no risk of the fire spreading. **Ratio: The moot point is whether the accused *intended or was reckless* as to whether life might have been endangered, not whether life was *actually* endangered. Application:** Dismissing the Defendant's appeal against conviction, the Court of Appeal said the ordinary prudent bystander without the benefit of hindsight or expert knowledge would have thought there was an obvious risk, and that was sufficient to establish recklessness.

MENS REA

General Principle: The danger to life must arise from damaged property.

R v Steer [1987] 2 All ER 833

Facts: A man fired a shot with an air rifle through a plate glass window, behind which people were standing; he was charged with aggravated criminal damage being reckless as to the danger to life. **Ratio: It was held that there had to be a causal link between the damage to property and the danger to life. Application:** His conviction was quashed by the Court of Appeal, and the House of Lords dismissed a further appeal by the prosecution: for this offence, said Lord Bridge, the Defendant must have intended or been reckless as to the danger to life resulting from the damage.

General Principle: Recklessness was considered to be the basis of conviction in this case.

R v Webster [1995] 2 All ER 168

Facts: The first Defendant and others threw stones from a railway bridge onto trains below; the second Defendant drove a stolen car and rammed a police car. The Defendants were separately convicted of aggravated criminal damage intending or being reckless as to a danger to life, and their appeals were dismissed. **Ratio: The Court reaffirmed the principle in Steer, but applied common sense to the facts of each case and said the Defendants were clearly reckless as to the possibility that their damage might lead to danger to life from the falling roof of the train, or to the crashing of the train or car and consequent danger to life. Application**: If the Defendant intended or was reckless that the stone would smash the roof of the train or vehicle so that metal or wood struts from the roof would or obviously might descend upon a passenger, endangering life, he would surely be guilty.

ARSON

It is criminal damage by the starting of a fire.

Section 1(3) of the 1971 Act provides:
Any offence committed under this section by destroying or damaging property by fire shall be charged as arson.

General Principle: The difference between this offence and the other forms of criminal damage is that the damage or destruction must be caused by a fire however slight.

R v Miller [1983] 1 All ER 978

Facts: A tramp took shelter in an empty house, and went to sleep with a cigarette in his hand. He awoke a little later to find that he had set the mattress alight, so he got up, went into another room, and went to sleep there. The fire took hold and the house burned down. **Ratio: Any criminal damage caused by fire will be categorised as arson. Application:** His conviction for arson was upheld by the House of Lords: having accidentally created the dangerous situation, he had a duty to take steps to remove the danger and his failure to do so was sufficient.

THREATS TO DESTROY OR DAMAGE PROPERTY

Under Section 2 of the Criminal Damage Act 1971, it is an offence to threaten to commit an offence under Section 1 of the Act. The maximum sentence is ten years' imprisonment.

Section 2 of the 1971 Act provides:
A person who without lawful excuse makes to another a threat, intending that that other would fear it would be carried out: (a) to destroy or damage property belonging to that other or a third person; or (b) to destroy or damage his own property in a way which he knows is likely to endanger the life of that other or third person; shall be guilty of an offence.

POSSESSION WITH INTENT TO DESTROY OR DAMAGE PROPERTY

It is an offence to be in possession of an article intending it to be used to commit an offence.

Section 3 of the 1971 Act provides:
A person who has anything in his custody or under his control intending without lawful excuse to use it or cause or permit another to use it: (a) to destroy or damage any property belong to some other person; or (b) to destroy or damage his own or the user's property in a way which he knows is likely to endanger the life of some other person; shall be guilty of an offence.

SUMMARY

- Two are the main offences created by the Criminal Damage Act 1971: simple criminal damage and aggravated criminal damage.

- Whether the Defendant have destroyed or damaged a property belonging to another he will be guilty of criminal damage.

- Aggravated criminal damage represents the aggravated form of simple criminal damage; The maximum sentence is life imprisonment.

- It is criminal damage by fire.

- Under Section 2 of the Criminal Damage Act 1971, it is an offence to threaten to commit an offence under Section 1 of the Act. The maximum sentence is ten years' imprisonment.

- It is an offence to be in possession of an article intending it to be used to commit an offence.

Chapter 13 – Theft

INTRODUCTION

Theft is the most significant offence created by the Theft Act 1968, is in Section 1(1). The maximum imprisonment attracted by the offence is seven years.

THEFT

Appropriation of property belonging to another amounts to theft.

Theft Act 1968 Section 1(1):
A person is guilty of theft if he dishonestly appropriates property belonging to another with the intention of permanently depriving the other of it.

ACTUS REUS

Three are the elements that must be proved:

- appropriation;
- of a property
- belonging to another.

Appropriation is assumption by a person of the rights of an owner as stated in Section 3(1) of the Theft Act 1968.

General Principle: Appropriation includes taking property, destroying it, using it in an unauthorised way, selling it, offering to sell it, or refusing to return it after having come by it legally.

R v Morris [1983] 3 All ER 288
Facts: A man took goods from the shelves of a supermarket and replaced the price labels attached to them with other labels showing a lower price. At the checkout he was asked for and paid the lower price; he was then arrested and subsequently convicted

of theft. **Ratio: Any assumption of the rights of an owner amounts to an appropriation. Application:** Dismissing the Defendant's appeal (and a conjoined appeal in *Anderton v Burnside*, in which another defendant had been arrested after switching the labels but before paying) the House of Lords said it was enough to prove that a Defendant had assumed any of the rights of an owner. Taking goods from the shelf was not in itself an appropriation, said Lord Roskill, nor would switching price labels be an appropriation if it were done merely as a prank, but a combination of acts such as occurred in the instant case was an adverse interference with the owner's rights and that was enough.

General Principle: It is possible to assume the owner's rights even when the act is done with the 'owner's consent'.

Lawrence v Commissioner of Police [1971] 2 All ER 1253
Facts: An Italian visitor arrived at Victoria Station, and went up to a taxi driver and showed him an address. The taxi driver said it was a long and expensive journey, though the proper fare was actually about 50p. The victim got into the taxi and gave the defendant £1 but kept his wallet open; the defendant took a further £6 from the wallet without any objection from the victim. **Ratio: The definition of theft does not include the words "without the owner's consent", though genuine consent will usually negative dishonesty. Application:** The Defendant was charged with the theft of the £6, and his conviction was upheld by the House of Lords. Viscount Dilhorne said he was not inclined to read s.1(1) as if the words "without the owner's consent" were included; by omitting those words, Parliament had relieved the prosecution of the burden of showing the absence of consent. If the defendant had genuinely believed that the victim had knowingly agreed to pay far more than the proper fare, his appropriation would not have been dishonest, but there was ample evidence here to suggest the contrary.

General Principle: The Defendant can appropriate property even with the consent of the owner.

R v Gomez [1993] 1 All ER 1
Facts: The first Defendant was the assistant manager at a shop and asked the manager to supply goods in exchange for a stolen cheque presented by an accomplice, the second Defendant. The manager (who was not party to the fraud) agreed, and the first defendant was subsequently charged with the theft of the goods. **Ratio: The current position is that R v Morris still holds true for establishing the assumption of any rights of the owner amounts to appropriation however it is no longer good law for the assertion that it cannot be appropriation if there is the consent of the owner. Application:** Dismissing his appeal, the House of Lords considered the conflict between the decision in *Lawrence* (above) and certain dicta of Lord Roskill in *Morris*, and declared that *Lawrence* and *Dobson* had been correctly decided. The decision in *Lawrence* made it clear that the absence of consent was not essential to an appropriation, and while genuine consent would often negate dishonesty that was not so where consent was obtained by a trick. The fact that the defendant might alternatively have been charged with obtaining by deception (under s.15) was irrelevant.

General Principle: The Defendant can be charged with theft even in cases of a 'gift'.

R v Hinks [2000] 4 All ER 833
Facts: A woman was the carer of an older man of low intelligence, and persuaded him to make gifts to her totalling some £60,000. **Ratio: Whether the acquisition of an indefeasible title to property is capable of amounting to an appropriation of property belonging to another for the purposes of Section 1(1) of the Theft Act 1968, the Defendant will be found guilty. Application:** The jury found as a fact that the Defendant had acted dishonestly and convicted her of theft. The House of Lords affirmed the conviction, and said there can be an appropriation even where the victim gives the money voluntarily to the thief.

General Principle: Appropriation could be a continuing rather than an instantaneous act.

R v Hale (1978) 68 Cr App R 415
Facts: The Defendants entered the victim's house wearing masks. The first Defendant put his hand over the victim's mouth while the other Defendant went upstairs for the victim's jewellery. Before they left, they tied up the victim and threatened to harm her child if she phoned the police. **Ratio: The act was considered to be a continuing one. Application:** Dismissing their appeal against conviction, the Court of Appeal said the theft was a continuing act, and did not come to an end once the jewellery had been seized; the jury was entitled to find that the Defendants had used force at the time of the theft in order to enable them to complete the theft.

DEFENCE UNDER THE ACT

General Principle: A Defendant is exempted from the liability for theft where the Defendant purchases goods in good faith and for value and then later discovers that the seller had no title to the property but decides to keep it.

R v Adams [1993] Crim LR 72
Facts: A motor-cyclist bought some spare parts which he was told had come from a crash write-off. Two or three days later he noticed that some part numbers had been erased, and only then suspected that the parts might have been stolen. **Ratio: A mala fide intention precludes the protection afforded by Section 3(2). Application:** He was acquitted of handling but convicted of theft on the basis of his later appropriation. The conviction was quashed on appeal: as a bona fide purchaser for value, he was entitled to the protection of Section 3(2).

PROPERTY

For the theft to be valid, the Defendant must have appropriated 'property' as established by **Section 4** of the Act.

General Principle: In order to establish that theft has taken place it is important to prove that the defendant has appropriated property.

Oxford v Moss (1978) 68 Cr App R 183
Facts: A student at Liverpool University obtained a copy of the examination paper he was due to sit. **Ratio: It was held that confidential information cannot fall within the definition of intangible property contained in Section 4(1). Application:** The property in question cannot be intangible. The Divisional Court affirmed his acquittal on a charge of stealing the confidential information contained in the paper (there being no proof that he intended to deprive the University of the paper itself).

General Principle: The property shall belong to someone else having any proprietary right or interest.

Williams v Phillips [1957] 41 Cr App R 5
Facts: The Defendants were dustmen employed by Bristol City Council, who took various items from bins (with the intention of selling them) before taking the rest of the rubbish to the tip. **Ratio: The householder intends the goods to be collected by the local authority, so a dustman could be guilty of theft if he appropriates goods from a dustbin with the relevant *mens rea*. Application:** The Divisional Court affirmed their convictions for larceny (theft): they knew quite well that saleable property was to be handed in and the proceeds divided. The rubbish was still the householder's property, until it became the property of the Council as soon as the dustmen arrived.

General Principle: The property can belong to persons who have possession or control not just of the specified property, but over the land upon which it was found.

R v Woodman [1974] 2 All ER 955
Facts: The Defendants took a van to a disused factory at Wick and loaded it with over a ton of scrap metal, which they took away. **Ratio: On the evidence, it was clear that the owners of the site**

were not aware that any usable scrap remained there, but the
Court of Appeal said the scrap was nonetheless their property
and upheld the Defendants' conviction. Application: Since the
factory owners had taken stepsto exclude trespassers there was
evidence that they were in control of the factory and thereby had
control of the scrap metal, which unknown to them had been left
inside the factory.

**General Principle: An owner can steal his own property if the
possession and control of the car was with someone else.**

R v Turner (No.2) [1971] 2 All ER 441
Facts: The Defendant took his car to a garage for repairs, and
when the garage had finished the work the car was parked in the
road outside. The Defendant told the garage he would return next
day to pay for the repairs and collect the car, but in fact he took it
that evening using his spare set of keys. **Ratio: An owner can be
charged with theft of his own property if the control of the car
was with another third party. Application:** He was charged
with the theft of the car, and his conviction was upheld by the
Court of Appeal; the car was in the "possession or control" of the
garage, and that made the car their property (as well as D's
property) for the time being. The jury was clearly satisfied as to
the defendant's dishonesty, and the conviction should stand.

**General Principle: The title in property passes at the time
that the parties intend it to pass.**

R v Hall [1972] 2 All ER 1009
Facts: Travel agents received money from customers and then
failed to arrange the promised holidays, using the money for their
own purposes. **Ratio: The Court of Appeal quashed the
Defendants' conviction for theft: the jury had not been asked
to decide whether the defendants were under an obligation to
account to the customers for the use of their money, or
whether they had merely failed to deliver the services for
which the customers had paid outright. Application:** The Court
of Appeal held that he was not guilty of theft because it was not
established that his clients expected him to retain and deal with

the money in a particular way, or that an obligation to do so was undertaken by him.

General Principle: A person in charge of a charity is plainly under an obligation to retain, if not the actual notes and coins, at least the proceeds collected for the charity.

R v Wain [1995] 2 Cr App R 660
Facts: The Defendant raised nearly £3000 from various events for the ITV Telethon. He paid the money into his personal bank account and drew on that a cheque in favour of the Telethon, but this and subsequent cheques bounced. **Ratio: McGowan LJ said that the Defendant had received money on behalf of the charity and had an obligation to hand over the equivalent sum, if not actually the same notes and coins. Instead, he had appropriated the money by using it for his own purposes. Application:** The Defendant was convicted of theft, and the Court of Appeal affirmed his conviction. When he took the money credited to that account and moved it over to his own bank account, it was still the proceeds of the notes and coins donated which he proceeded to use for his own purposes, thereby appropriating them.

MENS REA

The Defendant must have the intention to permanently deprive the other of the property.

Section 2(1) sets out three situations in which the defendant will not be held to be dishonest:

S2(1)(a) a defendant who believes he has in law the right to deprive the other of the property either for himself or another will not be dishonest.

S2(1)(b) a defendant who believes the person to whom the property belongs, would have consented had he known of the appropriation and the circumstances of the appropriation will not be dishonest.

S2(1)(c) a defendant who believes that the person to whom the property belongs cannot be discovered by taking reasonable steps will not be dishonest. There is no need for him to take reasonable steps, it is only necessary to believe that such steps will not enable him to find the owner.

General Principle: It is for the jury to decide whether what was done was dishonest according to ordinary standards of reasonable and honest people.

R v Ghosh [1982] 2 All ER 689
Facts: A locum surgeon claimed fees not actually due to him. He was charged with obtaining property by deception. **Ratio: The Court of Appeal said his conduct should be regarded as dishonest if (i) it would be considered dishonest by ordinary reasonable and honest people, and (ii) the Defedant was aware of that fact. Application:** Whether the Defendant himself thought his conduct dishonest, they said, was irrelevant. It is dishonest for a Defendant to act in a way which he knows ordinary people to consider being dishonest, even if he asserts or genuinely believes that he is morally justified in acting as he did.

General Principle: The Defendant must have the intention to permanently deprive the owner of his property at the time of the appropriation.

R v Lloyd [1985] 2 All ER 661
Facts: A cinema projectionist borrowed films without authority from his place of work so that friends could make pirate copies. **Ratio: The Defendants must have an intention of permanently depriving the owners of their property. Application:** The Defendant and the others were charged with conspiracy to steal, but their appeals against conviction were allowed by the Court of Appeal. They did not intend to deprive the owners of the films for more than a few hours, and when the films were returned they would still be just as usable as they were before.

General Principle: The defendant treats the thing as his own.

R v Fernandez [1996] 1 Cr App R 175

Facts: Fernandes was a solicitor who transferred money out of his clients' accounts and invested it in a risky money lending business. The money was lost. He claimed not to have had an intention to permanently deprive as he intended to return the money. He appealed unsuccessfully against his conviction for theft. **Ratio: The Court of Appeal said the critical notion in Section 6 is the Defendant's intention to treat the thing as his own regardless of the owner's rights: the second half of Section 6(1), and Section 6(2), are merely specific illustrations of this principle and there could be others. Application:** It was held in the case, "Section 6 may apply to a person in possession or control of another's property who, dishonestly and for his own purpose, deals with that property in such a manner that he knows he is risking its loss".

General Principle: 'To dispose of' could include 'dealing with the property' and that using the definition of 'to get rid of, or sell' was too narrow.

DPP v Lavender [1994] Crim LR 297

Facts: A man took two doors from a council house and used them to replace damaged doors in his girlfriend's house, owned by the same council. **Ratio: Section 6 may apply to a person in possession or control of another's property who, dishonestly and for his own purpose, deals with that property in such a manner that he knows he is risking its loss. Application:** The justices dismissed a charge of theft since he had not shown any intention permanently to deprive the council of their property. On appeal by the Crown, the Divisional Court remitted the case with a direction to convict: under the first limb of Section 6(1) the Defendant had treated the doors as his own to dispose of regardless of the owner's rights, and that was enough.

SUMMARY

- Theft is the dishonest appropriation of property belonging to another with intention of permanently depriving the other of it.

- Appropriation is any assumption of the rights of an owner, whether or not the owner has consented.

- Property includes money and all other property real or personal, including things in action and intangible things.

- The property must belong to another.

- The Ghosh Test is the one applied to assess dishonesty.

- The *mens rea* required bases on the intention to permanently deprive another of the property.

Chapter 14 - Robbery & Blackmail

ROBBERY

Robbery is an offence under Section 8 of the Theft Act 1968. Robbery is theft aggravated by use or threat of force.

Section 8 Theft Act 1968 provides:

(1) A person is guilty of robbery if he steals, and immediately before or at the time of doing so, and in order to do so, he uses force on any person or puts or seeks to put any person in fear of being then and there subjected to force. (2) A person guilty of robbery, or of an assault with intent to rob, shall on conviction on indictment be liable to imprisonment for life.

ACTUS REUS & MENS REA

In order to establish the actus reus of robbery there must be:

- theft
- force or fear of force
- immediately before or at the time of the theft
- applied in order to steal

The Defendant must act dishonestly and must intend to permanently deprive the other of the property.

General Principle: Robbery is an aggravated form of theft hence to make out the offence of robbery all the elements of theft must be fulfilled.

R v Robinson [1977] Crim LR 173
Facts: The Defendant ran a clothing club. He was charged, *inter alia*, with robbery from another person who contributed, with his wife, to the club. The Defendant and two others approached the victim, whose wife owed £7 to the club. A fight ensued and the defendant brandished a knife. A £5 note fell from the pocket of the victim. The defendant took the note and asked for £2 more.

The defendant's defence at court was that he was not dishonest because he received the money as payment for the debt. **Ratio: If the Defendant believed that he had the legal right to take the property then this will act as a defence. Application:** His conviction was quashed on the grounds that the trial judge had failed to direct the jury that he was entitled to an acquittal if he believed he had the legal right to take the property.

General Principle: A person is guilty of robbery if he steals and immediately before or at the time of doing so, and in order to do so, he uses or threatens force on any person.

R v Dawson & James [1976] 64 Cr App R 170
Facts: The Defendants approached the victim, and two of them nudged him from side to side while the third took the victim's wallet from his pocket. **Ratio: The amount of force used or threatened may have been small, and it is up to the jury to decide whether it was enough to constitute robbery. Application:** The word used in the statute was force, not violence and that is a question of fact. The Court of Appeal affirmed their conviction for robbery.

General Principle: The threat or use of force is immediately before or at the time of stealing.

R v Hale [1978] 68 Cr App R 415
Facts: The Defendants entered the victim's house wearing masks. The first Defendant put his hand over the victim's mouth while the second Defendant went upstairs for the victim's jewellery. Before they left, they tied up the victim and threatened to harm her child if she phoned the police. **Ratio: Dismissing their appeal against conviction, the Court of Appeal said the theft was a continuing act, and did not come to an end once the jewellery had been seized; the jury was entitled to find that the defendants had used force at the time of the theft in order to enable them to complete the theft. Application:** The court dismissed the appeal and held that the appropriation should be regarded as a continuing act. It was for the jury to decide when the act of appropriation had come to an end.

BLACKMAIL

It is a statutory offence regulated by Section 21 of the Theft Act 1968.

Section 21 of the 1968 Act:

(1)A person is guilty of blackmail if, with a view to gain for himself or another or with intent to cause loss to another, he makes any unwarranted demand with menaces; and for this purpose a demand with menaces is unwarranted unless the person making it does so in the belief— (a) that he has reasonable grounds for making the demand; and (b) that the use of the menaces is a proper means of reinforcing the demand. (2) The nature of the act or omission demanded is immaterial, and it is also immaterial whether the menaces relate to action to be taken by the person making the demand. (3) A person guilty of blackmail shall on conviction on indictment be liable to imprisonment for a term not exceeding fourteen years.

ACTUS REUS & MENS REA

The elements that need to be proved are:

- the presence of a demand
- which is unwarranted and
- made with menaces
- with a view to gain or loss.

The Defendant must be acting with a view to gain for himself or another or with intent to cause loss to another.

General Principle: The demand need not be express but can be implied from conduct and circumstances.

R v Collister & Warhurst [1955] 39 Cr App R 100
Facts: Two police officers intimated to the complainant that he was to be prosecuted for an offence. They asked him to meet them the next day while stating that the report of the offence will not occur if he fails to turn up for the meeting. At the meeting, one the defendants asked the complainant if he had anything for him. The complainant handed over £5. The defendants were convicted of blackmail and they claimed that they did not make any demands. **Ratio: The demand can be implied it does not have to be explicit. Application:** The Court upheld the convictions. The demeanour of the accused and the circumstances of the case were such that an ordinary reasonable man would understand that a demand for money was being made upon him.

General Principle: The threat of violence can be implied if it is not explicitly stated.

R v Lawrence and Pomroy [1971] 57 Cr App R 64
Facts: Pomroy repaired Mr Thorn's roof but he was not happy with it and refused to pay the full price. Pomroy demanded the remaining £70 and told him to 'keep looking over his shoulder' if he stepped out of the house. Pomroy returned to the house a few days later with Lawrence (a large man) and asked Mr Thorn to 'step outside' to sort matters out. **Ratio: The demand can be expressed or implied. Application:** Lawrence and Pomroy were charged with blackmail. They appealed on the ground that they had made of threat. The appeal was dismissed. The Court opined that the threat of violence can be implied and it need not be explicitly stated.

General Principle: It becomes an offence as soon as the demand is made there is no need to wait for the consequences.

Treacy v DPP [1971] 1 All ER 110
Facts: A man wrote and posted in England a letter addressed to another person in Germany, demanding money and threatening to tell her husband of her adultery if she did not pay. The Defendant was convicted of blackmail, but appealed on the grounds that the offence had not been committed in England so that the courts had

exceeded their jurisdiction. **Ratio: As regards the courts' jurisdiction, said Lord Diplock, where a crime involves both an act and a consequence it is enough that either the act or the consequence occur within England and Wales. But in any event, in the ordinary meaning of the language a person "makes a demand" as soon as he speaks or writes the relevant words; there is no need to wait for any consequence. Application:** The House of Lords by a majority upheld the Defendant's conviction.

General Principle: The demand must be such that the victim should actually be 'put in fear' that force will be used against him or at the very least apprehend that fact.

R v Clear [1968] 1 All ER 74
Facts: A lorry driver had his lorry and its contents stolen, and the owners of the contents brought legal proceedings against the Defendant's employers for the value of the contents. The Defendant then went to his employers and demanded money not to give evidence (contradicting his original report) tending to make the company vicariously liable for the loss. The company reported this to the police, and the defendant was charged with demanding money with menaces, contrary to the Larceny Act 1916. **Ratio: The Court of Appeal said the menaces must be such as to make it likely that a person of ordinary firmness would accede to the demand; it is not necessary that the actual victim (who may be particularly strong-minded) was himself alarmed. Application**: The court upheld his conviction since the demand made the victim dread that force might be used against him if he did not accede to the demand of the defendant.

General Principle: The demand generally refers to a "gain" for the Defendant.

R v Bevans [1987] 87 Cr App R 64
Facts: A man was in severe pain from an old war injury, and called a doctor at 4.00 am. When the doctor arrived at the Defendant's home, the Defendant pulled a gun from his pocket and threatened to shoot the doctor unless he gave the Defendant an

injection of morphine to reduce the pain. The doctor had no morphine but gave the Defendant an injection of pethidine; the Defendant then calmed down and apologised for his behaviour. **Ratio: The demand must make the victim fearful for his life and it generally involves a gain for the Defendant. Application:** Upholding the Defendant's conviction for blackmail, Watkins LJ said his demand for morphine was a demand for property with a view to gain for himself, the gain being relief from pain.

SUMMARY

- Robbery is an offence under Section 8 of the Theft Act 1968. Robbery is theft aggravated by use or threat of force.

- The force or fear of force must be applied immediately before or at the time of the theft with the purpose to steal.

- The Defendant must act dishonestly and must intend to permanently deprive the other of the property.

- Blackmail is a demand which is unwarranted and made with menaces with a view to gain or cause the loss of another.

Chapter 15 - Burglary

BURGLARY

A person is guilty of burglary whether he enters a building or part of a building as a trespasser with intent to steal, inflict grievous bodily harm, do unlawful damage OR whether having entered a building or part of a building as a trespasser, he steals/attempts to steal or inflicts/attempts to inflict grievous bodily harm.

Section 9 *Theft Act 1968:*

(1) A person is guilty of burglary if - (a) he enters any building or part of a building as a trespasser and with intent to commit any such offence as is mentioned in subsection (2) below; or (b) having entered any building or part of a building as a trespasser he steals or attempts to steal anything in the building or that part of it or inflicts or attempts to inflict on any person any grievous bodily harm.(2) The offences referred to in subsection (1)(a) above are offences of stealing anything in the building or part of a building in question, of inflicting on any person therein any grievous bodily harm and of doing unlawful damage to the building or anything therein. (3) A person guilty of burglary shall on conviction on indictment be liable to imprisonment for a term not exceeding - (a) where the offence was committed in respect of a building or part of a building which is a dwelling, fourteen years; (b) in any other case, ten years. (4) References in subsections (1) and (2) above to a building, and the reference to subsection (3) above to a building which is a dwelling, shall apply also to an inhabited vehicle or vessel, and shall apply to any such vehicle or vessel at times when the person having a habitation in it is not there as well as at times when he is.

ACTUS REUS

General Principle: The prosecution must establish that the Defendant 'enters' a building or a part of a building.

R v Collins [1972] 2 All ER 1105

Facts: Early one summer morning the Defendant climbed up a ladder to a young woman's bedroom window, intending to have sex with her whether she consented or not. As he crouched on the windowsill the woman woke up and saw the dim figure of a naked man. Assuming it was her boyfriend, she beckoned him into her bed and they had sex together. Eventually the woman realised it was not her boyfriend at all, whereupon she slapped his face and fled. **Ratio: Entry is established if the whole body of the person enters a building. Application:** The Defendant was charged with burglary with intent to rape. Quashing his conviction, the Court of Appeal said there must be "an effective and substantial entry" into the building without the complainant doing or saying anything to cause him to believe that she was consenting to his entering it, he ought not to be convicted of the offence charged.

General Principle: The entry must be 'effective', it will be considered entry even if the whole body of the person in not inside the building.

R v Brown [1985] Crim LR 212

Facts: The Defendant was arrested while standing on the pavement outside a shop, with his upper body and arms through a broken window as he rummaged through the goods inside.

Ratio: The Court said that the word substantial' did not materially assist, but the entry must be "effective". In this case, entry was "effective". Application: His conviction for burglary was upheld by the Court of Appeal, who said this was sufficient entry as long as the ulterior intent was present. This marks a change from the earlier decision.

General Principle: It is for the jury to decide whether there has been an 'entry' or not.

R v Ryan [1996] Crim LR 320

Facts: The Defendant was found trapped in a window frame, with his head and one arm inside the house and the rest of him outside.

Ratio: The Court held that it was irrelevant whether or not the accused was capable of stealing anything as a result of his entry. The act of entry need not, therefore, be either an

"effective" or a "substantial" entry. Rather it seems that it is a matter for the jury to decide whether there has been an "entry". **Application:** His appeal against his conviction for burglary was dismissed; even though he could not in fact steal anything because of being stuck, his entry was sufficient. This sets down the current position of law.

General Principle: What constitutes a 'building' is a question of fact.

B and S v Leathley [1979] Crim LR 314
Facts: The case involved a freezer container which was used to store frozen foods which was detached from its chassis and was resting on railway sleepers. It had been in position for two years and was fitted with electricity and was 25 feet long by seven feet square. **Ratio: It is a question of fact whether a place is a 'building' or not and must be decided by the jury.** **Application:** This was held to be a building in order to establish burglary.

General Principle: Entry into a building or part of a building is a trespass where the building or part entered is in the possession of another, who does not consent to the entry.

R v Jones & Smith [1976] 3 All ER 54
Facts: A boy and his friend into his father's house one night and stole two television sets. The father had told his son that he was welcome in the house any time, but both the Defendants were charged with burglary. **Ratio: Provided that the facts are known to the accused which enable him to realise that he is acting in excess of the permission given or that he is acting recklessly as to whether he exceeds that permission, then that is sufficient for the jury to decide that he is in fact a trespasser.** **Application:** The Court of Appeal affirmed their conviction; the jury was entitled to infer that the father would not have consented to the Defendant's entry for the purpose of stealing. [On this basis it would appear that every shoplifter is ipso facto a burglar, and the precedent should perhaps be treated with caution. However, it means that a person who gains access to a house by pretending to

be the gas inspector is a trespasser if he then uses the opportunity to steal.]

General Principle: Entry into "a dwelling with the intent to steal" is aggravated burglary (If it was a domicile, as opposed to a 'part of a building' as defined in section 9(1)(a) of the Theft Act of 1968.

R v Chipunza (Bruce) [2021] EWCA Crim 597
Facts: The defendant entered a hotel room with the intention of stealing. One of the accusations against him was burglary because he allegedly "entered a dwelling with the intent to steal" (If it was a domicile, as opposed to a 'part of a building' as defined in section 9(1)(a) of the Theft Act of 1968, he was culpable of aggravated burglary, which carries a harsher sentence.) He was convicted based on a directive that left it up to the jury to determine whether or not the hotel room was a domicile. **Ratio: The Court of Appeal, in overturning the conviction, ruled that the judge, when instructing the jury on the definition of a habitation for purposes of section 9(1)(a), should have explained what a dwelling was. Application:** It would have sufficed to say that a domicile was a building or part of a building in which a person lived and made their home; the most common examples of dwellings were houses and apartments in which people lived and made their homes, but other buildings or portions of buildings could also be considered dwellings. This should have been followed by a list of characteristics that the jury could have deemed indicative of whether or not the hotel room was a residence.

MENS REA

General Principle: If the Defendant would have an intention to steal at the point of entry, this satisfies the requirements under the section.

Attorney-General's Reference (Nos.1 & 2 of 1979) [1979] 3 All ER 143

Facts: If a person enters a building with an intention to simply look inside the property and steal only if there is anything worth stealing what happens in such a scenario. **Ratio: The Court of Appeal declared, on a point of law referred by the Attorney-General, that a person who enters a house intending to steal only if he finds money (or other valuable items) in the house can be convicted of burglary contrary to Section 9(1) of the Theft Act 1968 notwithstanding that his intention to steal is conditional. Application:** Even if the Defendant's intention to steal is conditional it satisfies the requirements of this offence.

DIFFERENCE BETWEEN BURGLARY UNDER SECTION 9(1)(A) AND SECTION 9(1)(B)

The only difference is that under Section 9(1)(a) burglary, the Defendant must enter as a trespasser with the intent to steal, inflict grievous bodily hurt or unlawfully damage property. Here, the burglary is committed at the point of entry. Under Section 9(1)(b) burglary, the defendant must enter as a trespasser and actually steal or attempt to steal or inflict grievous bodily hurt or unlawfully damage property. Here, the burglary is committed at the point of commission.

AGGRAVATED BURGLARY

Section 10 of the Theft Act 1968:
(1) A person is guilty of aggravated burglary if he commits any burglary and at the time has with him any firearm or imitation firearm, any weapon of offence, or any explosive; and for this purpose - (a) 'firearm' includes an airgun or airpistol, and 'imitation firearm' means anything which has the appearance of being a firearm, whether capable of being discharged or not; and (b) 'weapon of offence' means any article made or adapted for use for causing injury to or incapacitating a person, or intended by the person having it with him for such use; and (c) 'explosive' means any article manufactured for the purpose of producing a practical effect by explosion, or intended by the person having it with him for that purpose. (2) A person guilty of aggravated

burglary shall on conviction on indictment be liable to imprisonment for life.

General Principle: It is important to establish that the defendant had the offending article with him at the time of committing the burglary.

R v O'Leary [1986] 82 Cr App R 341
Facts: The Appellant forced entry into a private house when he was unarmed. He then picked up a knife from the kitchen and went upstairs where he confronted the two occupants. He committed a theft and injured the occupants. In answer to a charge of Section 9(1) (b) aggravated burglary the appellant claimed he could not be guilty because he was not armed when he entered the house. **Ratio: The Court of Appeal held that the time when he must have the weapon of offence was the time at which he actually stole. In this case, that was when he confronted the householders and demanded their cash. Application:** Hence, even though he did not enter the house with the weapon, he had it with him when he committed the burglary.

General Principle: Even though the Defendant entered the house with the weapon his intention to steal at the point of entry must be established.

R v Francis [1982] Crim LR 363
Facts: The Defendants, who were armed with sticks, were allowed by the victim to enter after they noisily demanded entry. They then discarded their sticks and subsequently stole articles from the house. **Ratio: The Defendants' intention to steal at the point of entry must be established to satisfy the requirements of this offence. Application:** Their convictions for aggravated burglary were quashed; they may have entered with weapons of offence but there was no evidence that at the point of entry they intended to steal.

SUMMARY

- A person is guilty of burglary whether he enters a building or part of a building as a trespasser with intent to steal, inflict grievous bodily harm, do unlawful damage OR whether having entered a building or part of a building as a trespasser, he steals/attempts to steal or inflicts/attempts to inflict grievous bodily harm.

- The offence is defined by Section 9 of the Theft Act 1968.

- A person is guilty of aggravated burglary if he commits any burglary and at the time has with him any firearm or imitation firearm, any weapon of offence, or any explosive.

Chapter 16 - Fraud

OVERVIEW

INTRODUCTION

The Fraud Act 2006, which came into force on 15 January 2007, abolished the old deception offences, replacing them with a new offence of fraud, which can be committed in many different ways.

FRAUD BY FALSE REPRESENTATION

Section 2 of the Fraud Act 206 makes it an offence to commit fraud by false representation. The representation must be made dishonestly.

The Fraud Act Section 2 provides:

(1) A person is in breach of this section if he (a) dishonestly makes a false representation, and (b) intends, by making the representation (i) to make a gain for himself or another, or (ii) to cause loss to another or to expose another to a risk of loss.

ACTUS REUS

According to **Section 2**:

(2) A representation is false if (a) it is untrue or misleading ... (3) "Representation" means any representation as to fact or law, including a representation as to the state of mind of— (a) the person making the representation, or (b) any other person. (4) A representation may be express or implied.

General Principle: The representation that forms the foundation of the case can be made clearly by the Defendant, or can be implied.

R v King [1979] Crim LR (122)

Facts: A second-hand car dealer stated that the mileage reading on a particular car 'may not be correct'. **Ratio: The representation can be expressed or implied. Application:** The court held that the Defendant had impliedly represented that he was not certain the reading was wrong (in fact he knew it was wrong as he had altered it). The latter representation is one of present fact, about the dealer's mental state.

General Principle: If the Defendant is in a better position to express the belief or opinion than the other party this may also amount to a false representation.

Smith v Land and House Property Corp (1884) 28 Ch D 7

Facts: A hotel was advertised hotel for sale by auction. Smith said that the whole of the property was let to Mr Fleck, *"a most desirable tenant"* at a rent of £400 per year for the next 27 years. Before the conveyance could take place, Fleck went bankrupt, and the corporation refused to go ahead with the sale. **Ratio: If the facts are not equally well known to both sides, then a statement of opinion by the one who knows the facts best involves very often a statement of material fact, for he impliedly states that he knows facts which justify his opinion. Application:** Hence, if the Defendant was in a better position to know something then his opinion will amount to false representation if it is false or untrue or misleading.

FRAUD BY OVERCHARGING

Whether the Defendant unfairly and knowingly overcharges a person, he will guilty of fraud by overcharging.

General Principle: In these cases, the Defendants take advantage of the vulnerability of the complainants and make false representations to overcharge.

R v Silverman (1988) 86 Cr App R 213

Facts: A builder who had worked for the family of two sisters for several years charged excessive amounts for work done on the home. **Ratio: A false representation arose because of 'circumstances of mutual trust'. Application:** The Court held that in such circumstances of mutual trust, one party depending upon the other for fair and reasonable conduct, the criminal law may apply if one party takes dishonest advantage of the other by representing as a fair charge that which he but not the other knows is dishonestly excessive.

MENS REA

General Principle: It is for the jury to decide whether what was done was dishonest according to ordinary standards of reasonable and honest people.

R v Ghosh [1982] 2 All ER 689
Facts: A locum surgeon claimed fees not actually due to him. He was charged with obtaining property by deception. **Ratio: The Court of Appeal said his conduct should be regarded as dishonest if (i) it would be considered dishonest by ordinary reasonable and honest people, and (ii) the defendant was aware of that fact. Whether the defendant himself thought his conduct dishonest, they said, was irrelevant. Application:** It is dishonest for a Defendant to act in a way which he knows ordinary people to consider being dishonest, even if he asserts or genuinely believes that he is morally justified in acting as he did.

General Principle: There must be an intention to make a gain or cause a loss

However, this element of *mens rea* is much wider than that: it is enough that the Defendant intends to make a gain for himself or for someone else, or that he intends to cause a loss to another, or even just expose someone to a risk of loss.

Section 5 of the Fraud Act:
(2) 'Gain' and 'loss'—(a) extend only to gain or loss in money or other property; (b) include any such gain or loss whether

temporary or permanent; and "property" means any property whether real or personal (including things in action and other intangible property). (3) "Gain" includes a gain by keeping what one has, as well as a gain by getting what one does not have. (4) "Loss" includes a loss by not getting what one might get, as well as a loss by parting with what one has.

FRAUD BY FAILURE TO DISCLOSE

Failing to disclose information may cause liability whether the Defendant acted dishonestly intending to make a gain The defendant must be under a legal duty to disclose the information.

Section 3 of the Fraud Act:
A person is in breach of this section if he— (a) dishonestly fails to disclose to another person information which he is under a legal duty to disclose, and (b) intends, by failing to disclose the information— (i) to make a gain for himself or another, or (ii) to cause loss to another or to expose another to a risk of loss.

FRAUD BY ABUSE OF POSITION

This is when someone abuses their position of authority or trust against another person for personal or financial gain, or to cause loss to another.

Section 4 of the Fraud Act:
(1) A person is in breach of this section if he— (a) occupies a position in which he is expected to safeguard, or not to act against, the financial interests of another person, (b) dishonestly abuses that position, and (c) intends, by means of the abuse of that position— (i) to make a gain for himself or another, or (ii) to cause loss to another or to expose another to a risk of loss. (2) A person may be regarded as having abused his position even though his conduct consisted of an omission rather than an act.

General Principle: It is for the jury to decide whether what was done was dishonest according to ordinary standards of reasonable and honest people.

R v Ghosh [1982] 2 All ER 689
Facts: A locum surgeon claimed fees not actually due to him. He was charged with obtaining property by deception. **Ratio: It is dishonest for a Defendant to act in a way which he knows ordinary people to consider being dishonest, even if he asserts or genuinely believes that he is morally justified in acting as he did. Application:** The Court of Appeal said his conduct should be regarded as dishonest if (i) it would be considered dishonest by ordinary reasonable and honest people, and (ii) the Defendant was aware of that fact. Whether the defendant himself thought his conduct dishonest, they said, was irrelevant.

MAKING OFF WITHOUT PAYMENT

Making off without payment **is** an offence under Section 3 Theft Act 1978.

Section 3 of the Theft Act 1978:
A person who, knowing that payment on the spot for any goods supplied or services done is required or expected from him, dishonestly makes off without having paid as required or expected and with intent to avoid payment of the amount shall be guilty of an offence.

General Principle: The requirement is that the Defendant leaves the place at which payment is required.

R v McDavitt [1981] Crim LR 843
Facts: The Defendant refused to pay his bill in a restaurant after having an argument with the manager. He tried to walk out of the restaurant but the manager told him the police had been called and told him to stay. He stayed till the police came and was charged with making off without payment. **Ratio: The offence was not made out because he had not left the restaurant and had not 'made-off'. Application:** Leaving the place of payment is important for the offence to be made out.

MENS REA

General Principle: There must be knowledge that payment is required or expected.

Troughton v Metropolitan Police [1987] Crim LR 138
Facts: A taxi-driver had agreed to drive the drunken Defendant home. He stopped to get better directions from the Defendant. There was an argument and the Defendant accused the taxi driver of taking a diversion to increase the fare. The taxi-driver, being unable to obtain a proper destination drove the defendant to the police station. **Ratio: If the contract is not fulfilled the need for payment will not arise. Application:** The Defendant was charged with making off without payment and he appealed. The Court allowed the appeal and held that as the journey was not yet complete, the taxi driver was in breach of contract in not taking the Defendant home, and therefore no lawful demand for payment could be made or avoided.

General Principle: There must be an intention to avoid payment.

R v Allen [1985] AC 1029
Facts: Allen stayed at a hotel for around a month and left without paying the bill. He telephoned the hotel and said he was experiencing financial difficulties as he was awaiting payment from certain business transactions. He arranged to pick up his belongings and to leave his passport to secure the debt. When he went to pick up his things the police were waiting for him and arrested him. **Ratio: If the Defendant intended to pay even at a later stage then he does not fulfil the requirements of this offence. Application:** The jury convicted and the Appellant appealed contending that an intention to temporarily avoid payment was not within the ambit of the Act. On appeal, the conviction was quashed and it was held that making off without payment required an intention to permanently avoid payment.

SUMMARY

- The Fraud Act 2006, which came into force on 15 January 2007, abolished the old deception offences, replacing them with a new offence of fraud.

- **Section 2** of the Fraud Act 206 makes it an offence to commit fraud by false representation.

- Whether the Defendant unfairly or knowingly overcharges a person, he will guilty of fraud by overcharging.

- Failing to disclose information may cause liability whether the Defendant acted dishonestly intending to make a gain. The defendant must be under a legal duty to disclose the information.

- Fraud by abusing of position is when someone abuses their position of authority or trust against another person for personal or financial gain, or to cause loss to another.

- Making off without payment **is** an offence under Section 3 Theft Act 1978.

www.ingramcontent.com/pod-product-compliance
Lightning Source LLC
LaVergne TN
LVHW052241150726
843469LV00054B/2170